NYSTCE

080

Communication and Quantitative Skills

Teacher Certification Exam

By: Sharon Wynne, M.S.
Southern Connecticut State University

"And, while there's no reason yet to panic, I think it's only prudent that we make preparations to panic."

XAMonline, INC.
Boston

Library of Congress Cataloging-in-Publication Data

Wynne, Sharon A.
    CQST Communication and Quantitative Skills 080: Teacher Certification
    / Sharon A. Wynne. -2nd ed. ISBN: 978-1-58197-865-0
        1. CQST Communication and Quantitative Skills 080.   2. Study Guides.
        3. NYSTCE   4. Teachers' Certification & Licensure.   5. Careers

Disclaimer:

The opinions expressed in this publication are the sole works of XAMonline and were created independently from the National Education Association, Educational Testing Service, or any State Department of Education, National Evaluation Systems or other testing affiliates.

Between the time of publication and printing, state specific standards as well as testing formats and website information may change that is not included in part or in whole within this product. Sample test questions are developed by XAMonline and reflect similar content as on real tests; however, they are not former tests. XAMonline assembles content that aligns with state standards but makes no claims nor guarantees teacher candidates a passing score. Numerical scores are determined by testing companies such as NES or ETS and then are compared with individual state standards. A passing score varies from state to state.

Printed in the United States of America   œ-1

NYSTCE: CQST Communication and Quantitative Skills 080
ISBN: 978-1-58197-865-0

Table of Contents

Study and Testing Tips

In the preface, emphasis was placed upon the idea of focusing on the right material, in other words, *what* to study in order to prepare for the subject assessments. But equally important is *how* you study.

learning n. 1. the acquiring of knowledge of or skill in (a subject, trade, art, etc.) by study; experience, etc. 2. to come to know (of or about) 3. acquired knowledge or skill. *(Definition courtesy of Webster's New World Dictionary of the American Language, 1987)*

What we call learning is actually a very complicated process built around multi-faceted layers of sensory input and reinforcement. When you were a child, learning largely consisted of trial and error experimentation, (i.e., "Don't touch that," "It's *Hot!*" or "This tastes *Good!*").

But as we grow older and the neurotransmitters within our brain develop, learning takes on deeper, subtler levels. As adults the neural pathways are fully in place, allowing us to make abstract connections, synthesizing all of our previous experiences (which is essentially what knowledge is), into tremendously complicated, cohesive thoughts.

However, you can increase your chances of truly mastering the information by taking some simple, but effective steps.

Study Tips:

1. **Some foods aid the learning process.** Foods such as milk, nuts, seeds, rice, and oats help your study efforts by releasing natural memory enhancers called CCKs (*cholecystokinin*) composed of *tryptophan*, *choline*, and *phenylalanine*. All of these chemicals enhance the neurotransmitters associated with memory. Before studying, try a light, protein-rich meal of eggs, turkey, and fish. All of these foods release the memory enhancing chemicals. The better the connections, the more you comprehend.

   Likewise, before you take a test, stick to a light snack of energy boosting and relaxing foods. A glass of milk, a piece of fruit, or some peanuts all release various memory-boosting chemicals and help you to relax and focus on the subject at hand.

2. **Learn to take great notes.** A by-product of our modern culture is that we have grown accustomed to getting our information in short doses (i.e. TV news sound bites or USA Today style newspaper articles.)

Consequently, we've subconsciously trained ourselves to assimilate information better in neat little packages. If your notes are scrawled all over the paper, it fragments the flow of the information. Strive for clarity.

Newspapers use a standard format to achieve clarity. Your notes can be much clearer through use of proper formatting. A very effective format is called the *Cornell Method*. Take a sheet of loose-leaf lined notebook paper and draw a line all the way down the paper about 1-2" from the left-hand edge. Draw another line across the width of the paper about 1-2" up from the bottom. Repeat this process on the reverse side of the page.

Look at the highly effective result. You have ample room for notes, a left hand margin for special emphasis items or inserting supplementary data from the textbook, a large area at the bottom for a brief summary, and a little rectangular space for just about anything you want.

3. **Dissect the material.** Too often we focus on the details and donâ€™t gather an understanding of the concept. However, if you simply memorize only dates, places, or names, you may well miss the whole point of the subject.

A key way to understand things is to put them in your own words. If you are working from a textbook, automatically summarize each paragraph in your mind. If you are outlining text, don't simply copy the author's words. *Rephrase* them in your own words. You remember your own thoughts and words much better than someone else's, and subconsciously tend to associate the important details to the core concepts.

4. **Turn every heading and caption in to a question.** Pull apart written material paragraph by paragraph and don't forget the captions under the illustrations.

Example: If the heading is "Stream Erosion", flip it around to read "Why do streams erode?" Then answer the questions.

If you train your mind to think in a series of questions and answers, not only will you learn more, but it also helps to lessen the test anxiety because you are used to answering questions.

5. <u>**Read, Read, Read.**</u> Even if you only have 10 minutes, put your notes or a book in your hand. Your mind is similar to a computer; you have to input data in order to have it processed. *By reading, you are storing data for future retrieval.* The more times you read something, the more you reinforce the storage of data.

   Even if you don't fully understand something on the first pass, *your mind stores much of the material for later recall.*

6. <u>**Create the right study atmosphere.**</u> Our bodies respond to an inner clock called biorhythms. Burning the midnight oil works well for some people, but not everyone. If possible, set aside a particular place to study that is free of distractions. Shut off the television, cell phone, pager and exile your friends and family during your study period.

   If you really are bothered by silence, try background music. Not rock, not hip-hop, not country, but classical. Light classical music at a low volume has been shown to aid in concentration. Don't pick anything with lyrics; you end up singing along. Try just about anything by Mozart, generally light and airy, it subconsciously evokes pleasant emotions and helps relax you.

7. <u>**Limit the use of highlighters.**</u> At best, it's difficult to read a page full of yellow, pink, blue, and green streaks. Try staring at a neon sign for a while and you'll soon see my point, the horde of colors obscure the message. A quick note, a brief dash of color, an underline, and an arrow pointing to a particular passage is much clearer than a horde of highlighted words.

8. <u>**Budget your study time.**</u> Although you shouldn't ignore any of the material, ***allocate your available study time in the same ratio that topics may appear on the test.***

Testing Tips:

1. **Don't outsmart yourself.** Don't read anything into the question. Don't make an assumption that the test writer is looking for something else than what is asked. Stick to the question as written and don't read extra things into it.

2. **Read the question and all the choices** *twice* **before answering the question.** You may miss something by not carefully reading, and then re-reading both the question and the answers. If you really don't have a clue as to the right answer, leave it blank on the first time through. Go on to the other questions, as they may provide a clue as to how to answer the skipped questions. If later on, you still can't answer the skipped ones . . . *Guess.* The only penalty for guessing is that you *might* get it wrong. Only one thing is certain; if you don't put anything down, you will get it wrong!

3. **Turn the question into a statement.** Look at the way the questions are worded. The syntax of the question usually provides a clue. Does it seem more familiar as a statement rather than as a question? Does it sound strange? By turning a question into a statement, you may be able to spot if an answer sounds right, and it may also trigger memories of material you have read.

4. **Look for hidden clues.** It's actually very difficult to compose multiple-foil (choice) questions without giving away part of the answer in the options presented. In most multiple-choice questions you can often readily eliminate one or two of the potential answers. This leaves you with only two real possibilities and automatically your odds go to fifty-fifty for very little work.

5. **Trust your instincts.** For every fact that you have read, you subconsciously retain something of that knowledge. On questions that you aren't really certain about, go with your basic instincts, **your first impression on how to answer a question is usually correct.**

6. **Mark your answers directly on the test booklet.** Don't bother trying to fill in the optical scan sheet on the first pass through the test. Just be very careful not to miss-mark your answers when you eventually transcribe them to the scan sheet.

7. **Watch the clock!** You have a set amount of time to answer the questions. Don't get bogged down trying to answer a single question at the expense of 10 questions you can more readily answer

THIS PAGE BLANK

COMPETENCY 1.0   UNDERSTANDS THE MEANING OF GENERAL VOCABULARY WORDS

Skill 1.1   Determines the meaning of commonly encountered words presented in context

Context clues help reader determine the meaning of words they are not familiar with. The context of a word is the sentence or sentences that surround the word.

Read the following sentences and attempt to determine the meanings of the words in bold print.

> The **luminosity** of the room was so incredible that there was no need for lights.

>> If there was no need for lights then one must assume that the word luminosity has something to do with giving off light. The definition of luminosity is: the emission of light.

> Jamie could not understand Joe's feelings. His mood swings made understanding him somewhat of an **enigma.**

>> The fact that he could not be understood made him somewhat of a puzzle. The definition of enigma is: a mystery or puzzle.

Familiarity with word roots (the basic elements of words) and with prefixes can also help one determine the meanings of unknown words.

Following is a partial list of roots and prefixes. It might be useful to review these.

Root	Meaning	Example
aqua	water	aqualung
astro	star	astrology
bio	life	biology
carn	meat	carnivorous
circum	around	circumnavigate
geo	earth	geology
herb	plant	herbivorous
mal	bad	malicious
neo	new	neonatal
tele	distant	telescope

Prefix	Meaning	Example
un-	not	unnamed
re-	again	reenter
il-	not	illegible
pre-	before	preset
mis-	incorrectly	misstate
in-	not	informal
anti-	against	antiwar
de-	opposite	derail
post-	after	postwar
ir-	not	irresponsible

Reading in your spare time - newspapers, magazines, novels - can also help to increase your overall vocabulary.

Skill 1.2   Identifies appropriate synonyms or antonyms for words

Synonyms are words that have similar meanings. Sometimes, synonyms can be used in place of another word to make a draft more appealing or descriptive. Teachers should encourage their students to utilize appropriate synonyms when drafting or revising their work to expand the interest and imagery of a written work. Paper or computer thesauruses are helpful in incorporating synonyms into one's writing.

> Examples of synonyms:
> Happy – gay, joyful, ecstatic, content, cheerful
> Angry – irritated, fuming, livid, irate, annoyed
> Beautiful - gorgeous, attractive, striking

However, teachers should also alert students that sometimes one word can not be simply replaced by another just because it was listed as a synonym. Sometimes the meaning or the connotation will vary somewhat. For example, in the sentence "Harold was <u>angry</u> when his brother spilled finger paint on his book report." Replacing "angry" with "fuming" would be a better choice than "annoyed" as the words describe the situation a little differently. As teachers work with students, they can help students expand their vocabularies so students know which synonyms to use.

Antonyms are words that have opposite meanings. As with synonyms, thesauruses will help students identify words that are antonyms.

> Examples of antonyms:
> Sad – cheerful, delighted
> Angry - calm, content
> Beautiful – ugly, repulsive, hideous

Skill 1.3   Recognizes the correct use of commonly misused pairs of words (e.g., their/there, to/too)

Students frequently encounter problems with homonyms—words that are spelled and pronounced the same as another but that have different meanings such as *mean*, a verb, "to intend"; *mean* an adjective, "unkind"; and *mean* a noun or adjective, "average." These words are actually both homonyms and homographs (written the same way).

A similar phenomenon that causes trouble is heteronyms (also sometimes called heterophones), words that are spelled the same but have different pronunciations and meanings (in other words, they are homographs that differ in pronunciation or, technically, homographs that are not homophones). For example, the homographs *desert* (abandon) and *desert* (arid region) are heteronyms (pronounced differently); but *mean* (intend) and *mean* (average) are not. They are pronounced the same, or are homonyms.

Another similar occurrence in English is the capitonym, a word that is spelled the same but has different meanings when it is capitalized and may or may not have different pronunciations. Example: *polish* (to make shiny) and *Polish* (from Poland).

Some of the most troubling homonyms are those that are spelled differently but sound the same. Examples: *its* (3d person singular neuter pronoun) and *it's* ("it is"); *there, their* (3d person plural pronoun) and *they're* ("they are").

Others: *to, too, two;*

Some homonyms/homographs are particularly complicated and troubling. Fluke, for instance is a fish, a flatworm, the end parts of an anchor, the fins on a whale's tail, and a stroke of luck.

Common misused words:

Accept is a verb meaning to receive or to tolerate. **Except** is usually a preposition meaning excluding. Except is also a verb meaning to exclude.

Advice is a noun meaning recommendation. **Advise** is a verb meaning to recommend.

Affect is usually a verb meaning to influence. **Effect** is usually a noun meaning result. Effect can also be a verb meaning to bring about.

An **allusion** is an indirect reference. An **illusion** is a misconception or false impression.

Add is a verb to mean to put together. **Ad** is a noun that is the abbreviation for the word advertisement.

Ain't is a common nonstandard contraction for the contraction aren't.

Allot is a verb meaning to distribute. **A lot** can be an adverb that means often, or to a great degree. It can also mean a large quantity.

Allowed is used here as an adjective that means permitted. **Aloud** is an adverb that means audibly.

Bare is an adjective that means naked or exposed. It can also indicate a minimum. As a noun, **bear** is a large mammal. As a verb, bear means to carry a heavy burden.

Capitol refers to a city, and capitol to a building where lawmakers meet. **Capital** also refers to wealth or resources.

A **chord** is a noun that refers to a group of musical notes. **Cord** is a noun meaning rope or a long electrical line.

Compliment is a noun meaning a praising or flattering remark. **Complement** is a noun that means something that completes or makes perfect.

Climactic is derived from climax, the point of greatest intensity in a series or progression of events. **Climatic** is derived from climate; it refers to meteorological conditions.

Discreet is an adjective that means tactful or diplomatic, **discrete** is an adjective that means separate or distinct.

Dye is a noun or verb used to indicate artificially coloring something. **Die** is a verb that means to pass away. Die is also a noun that means a cube-shaped game piece.

Effect is a noun that means outcome. **Affect** is a verb that means to act or produce an effect on.

Elicit is a verb meaning to bring out or to evoke. **Illicit** is an adjective meaning unlawful

Emigrate means to leave one country or region to settle in another. **Immigrate** means to enter another country and reside there.

•

Horde is a verb that means to accumulate or store up. **Horde** is a large group.

Lead is a verb that means to guide or serve as the head of. It is also a noun that is a type of metal.

Medal is a noun that means an award that is strung round the neck. **Meddle** is a verb that means to involve oneself in a matter without right or invitation. **Metal** is an element such as silver or gold. **Mettle** is a noun meaning toughness or guts.

Morning is a noun indicating the time between midnight and midday. **Mourning** is a verb or noun pertaining to the period of grieving after a death.

Past is a noun meaning a time before now (past, present and future). **Passed** is the past tense of the verb "to pass."

Piece is a noun meaning a portion. **Peace** is a noun meaning the opposite of war.

Peak is a noun meaning the tip or height to reach the highest point. **Peek** is a verb that means to take a brief look. **Pique** is a verb meaning to incite or raise interest.

Principal is a noun meaning the head of a school or an organization or a sum of money. **Principle** is a noun meaning a basic truth or law.

Rite is a noun meaning a special ceremony. **Right** is an adjective meaning correct or direction. **Write** is a verb meaning to compose in writing.

Than is a conjunction used in comparisons; **then** is an adverb denoting time. That pizza is more <u>than</u> I can eat. Tom laughed, and <u>then</u> we recognized him.

Than is used to compare; both words have the letter a in them.

Then tells when; both are spelled the same, except for the first letter.

There is an adverb specifying place; it is also an expletive. Adverb: Sylvia is lying <u>there</u> unconscious. Expletive: <u>There</u> are two plums left. **Their** is a possessive pronoun. **They're** is a contraction of they are. Fred and Jane finally washed <u>their</u> car. <u>They're</u> later than usual today.

To is a preposition; **too** is an adverb; **two** is a number.

Your is a possessive pronoun; **you're** is a contraction of you are.

Strategies to help students conquer these demons: Practice using them in sentences. Context is useful in understanding the difference. Drill is necessary to overcome their misuses.

To effectively teach language, it is necessary to understand that, as human beings acquire language, they realize that words have denotative and connotative meanings. Generally, denotative words point to things and connotative words deal with mental suggestions that the words convey. The word skunk has a denotative meaning if the speaker can point to the actual animal as he speaks the word and intends the word to identify the animal. Skunk has connotative meanings depending upon the tone of delivery, the socially acceptable attitudes about the animal, and the speaker's personal feelings about the animal.

Problem Phrases

Correct	Incorrect
Supposed to	Suppose to
Used to	Use to
Toward	Towards
Anyway	Anyways
Couldn't care less	Could care less
For all intents and purposes	For all intensive purposes
Come to see me	Come and see me
En route	In route
Regardless	Irregardless
Second, Third	Secondly, Thirdly

Other confusing words

Lie is an intransitive verb meaning to recline or rest on a surface. Its principal parts are lie, lay, lain. **Lay** is a transitive verb meaning to put or place. Its principal parts are lay, laid.

> Birds lay eggs.
> I lie down for bed around 10 PM.

Set is a transitive verb meaning to put or to place. Its principal parts are set, set, set. **Sit** is an intransitive verb meaning to be seated. Its principal parts are sit, sat, sat.

> I set my backpack down near the front door.
> They sat in the park until the sun went down.

Among is a preposition to be used with three or more items. **Between** is to be used with two items.

> Between you and me, I cannot tell the difference among those three Johnson sisters.

As is a subordinating conjunction used to introduce a subordinating clause; **Like** is a preposition and is followed by a noun or a noun phrase.

> As I walked to the lab, I realized that the recent experiment findings were much like those we found last year.

Can is a verb that means to be able. **May** is a verb that means to have permission. They are only interchangeable in cases of possibility.

> I can light 250 pounds.
> May I go to Alex's house?

COMPETENCY 2.0   UNDERSTANDS THE STATED MAIN IDEA OF A READING PASSAGE

Skill 2.1   Identifies the stated main idea of a passage

A **topic** of a paragraph or story is what the paragraph or story is about.

The **main idea** of a paragraph or story states the important idea(s) that the author wants the reader to know about a topic.

The topic and main idea of a paragraph or story are sometimes directly stated.

There are times, however, that the topic and main idea are not directly stated, but simply implied.

> Look at this paragraph.

>> Henry Ford was an inventor who developed the first affordable automobile. The cars that were being built before Mr. Ford created his Model-T were very expensive. Only rich people could afford to have cars.

> The topic of this paragraph is Henry Ford. The main idea is that Henry Ford built the first affordable automobile.

Skill 2.2   Identifies the topic sentence of a passage

The **topic sentence** indicates what the passage is about. It is the subject of that portion of the narrative. The ability to identify the topic sentence in a passage will enable the student to focus on the concept being discussed and better comprehend the information provided.

You can find the main ideas by looking at the way in which paragraphs are written. A paragraph is a group of sentences about one main idea. Paragraphs usually have two types of sentences: a topic sentence, which contains the main idea, and two or more detail sentences which support, prove, provide more information, explain, or give examples.

You can only tell if you have a detail or topic sentence by comparing the sentences with each other.

Look at this sample paragraph:

Fall is the best of the four seasons. The leaves change colors to create a beautiful display of golds, reds, and oranges. The air turns crisp and windy. The scent of pumpkin muffins and apple pies fill the air. Finally, Halloween marks the start of the holiday season. Fall is my favorite time of year!

Breakdown of sentences:

Fall is the best of the four seasons. (TOPIC SENTENCE)
The leaves change colors to create a beautiful display of golds, reds, and oranges. (DETAIL)
The air turns crisp and windy. (DETAIL)
The scent of pumpkin muffins and apple pies fill the air. (DETAIL)
Finally, Halloween marks the start of the holiday season. (DETAIL)
Fall is my favorite time of year! (CLOSING SENTENCE – Often a restatement of the topic sentence)

The first sentence introduces the main idea and the other sentences support and give the many uses for the product.

Tips for Finding the Topic Sentence

1. The topic sentence is usually first, but could be in any position in the paragraph.

2. A topic is usually more "general" than the other sentences; that is, it talks about many things and looks at the big picture. Sometimes it refers to more that one thing. Plurals and the words "many", "numerous", or "several" often signal a topic sentence.

3. Detail sentences are usually more "specific" than the topic, that is, they usually talk about one single or small part or side of an idea. Also, the words "for example", "i.e.", "that is", "first", "second", "third", etc., and "finally" often signal a detail.

4. Most of the detail sentences support, give examples, prove, talk about, or point toward the topic in some way.

How can you be sure that you have a topic sentence? Try this trick: Switch the sentence you think is the topic sentence into a question. If the other sentences seem to "answer" the question, then you've got it.

For example:
Reword the topic sentence "Fall is the best of the four seasons" in one of the following ways:

"Why is fall the best of the four season?"
"Which season is the best season?"
"Is fall the best season of the year?"

Then, as you read the remaining sentences (the ones you didn't pick), you will find that they answer (support) your question.

If you attempt this with a sentence other than the topic sentence, it won't work

For example:
Suppose you select "Halloween marks the start of the holiday season," and you reword it in the following way:

"Which holiday is the start of the holiday season?"

You will find that the other sentences fail to help you answer (support) your question.

Skill 2.3   Recognizes introductory and summary statements of a passage

The introductory statement should be at the beginning of the passage. An introductory statement will provide a bridge between any previous, relevant text and the content to follow. It will provide information about, and set the tone and parameters for, the text to follow. The old axiom regarding presenting a body of information suggested that you should always "tell them what you are going to tell them; tell it to them; tell them what you just told them." The introductory statement is where the writer will tell the readers what he or she is going to tell them.

The summary statement should be at or near the end of the passage, and is a concise presentation of the essential data from that passage. In terms of the old axiom, the content portion (the main body of the narrative) is where the writer will "tell it to them." The summary statement is where the writer will tell the readers what he or she has just told them.

Skill 2.4   Selects an accurate restatement of the main idea of a passage

An accurate restatement of the main idea from a passage will usually summarize the concept in a concise manner, and it will often present the same idea from a different perspective. A restatement should always demonstrate complete comprehension of the main idea.

To select an accurate restatement, identifying the main idea of the passage is essential (see Skill 2.2). Once you comprehend the main idea of a passage, evaluate your choices to see which statement restates the main idea while eliminating statements which restate a supporting detail. Walk through the steps below the sample paragraph from Skill 2.2 to see how to select the accurate restatement.

Sample Paragraph:
Fall is the best of the four seasons. The leaves change colors to create a beautiful display of golds, reds, and oranges. The air turns crisp and windy. The scent of pumpkin muffins and apple pies fill the air. Finally, Halloween marks the start of the holiday season. Fall is my favorite time of year!

Steps:
1. Identify the main idea. (Answer: "Fall is the best of the four seasons.")
2. Decide which statement below restates the topic sentence:
   A. The changing leaves turn gold, red and orange.
   B. The holidays start with Halloween.
   C. Of the four seasons, Fall is the greatest of them all.
   D. Crisp wind is a fun aspect of Fall.

The answer is C because it rewords the main idea of the first sentence, the topic sentence.

COMPETENCY 3.0   UNDERSTANDS THE SEQUENCE OF IDEAS IN A READING PASSAGE

Skill 3.1   Identifies the order of events or steps described in a passage

The ability to organize events or steps provided in a passage (especially when presented in random order) serves a useful purpose, and it encourages the development of logical thinking and the processes of analysis and evaluation.

Working through and discussing with your students examples like the one below help students to gain valuable practice in sequencing events. In the example below, identify the proper order of events or steps:

Example:
1. Matt had tied a knot in his shoelace.
2. Matt put on his green socks because they were clean and complimented the brown slacks he was wearing.
3. Matt took a bath and trimmed his toenails.
4. Matt put on his brown slacks.

The proper order of events is: 3, 4, 2, and 1

Skill 3.2   Organizes a set of instructions into their proper sequence

Students need to be aware of their audience and how their writing comes across to their audience in order to write clearly and in a logical sequence. As with events or steps (discussed in Skill 3.1), the ability to organize a set of instructions into the proper sequence (especially when presented in random order) serves a useful purpose, and it encourages the development of logical thinking and the processes of analysis and evaluation.

Reading the example below proves to be quite confusing to the beginner cook. Proper sequence of events is crucial to ensuring that the meaning of the text is correctly interpreted by the reader. In the example below identify the proper sequence of instructions:

MAKING A YUMMY MACCARONI AND CHEESE DINNER FROM A PACKAGE IS FUN

1. I like mixing in the cheese because that is what makes the dinner so yummy.
2. You must bring the water to a boil in a pot before adding the macaroni.
3. Be sure to add a tablespoon of butter just after you put in the salt.
4. After you strain the cooked noodles, you return them to the pot and add a pinch of salt.
5. After the butter, add the quarter cup of milk.
6. Stir all the ingredients together until the powdered cheese has dissolved into a liquid which evenly coats the macaroni.
7. The macaroni will cook in the boiling water for ten minutes.
8. Of course, the cheese is the last ingredient added—just after the milk.
9. Serve in a big bowl and enjoy!

The proper sequence is: 2, 7, 4, 3, 5, 8, 6, 1, 9.

Skill 3.3   Identifies cause-and-effect relationships described in a passage

Linking cause to effect seems to be ingrained in human thinking. We get chilled and then the next day come down with a cold; therefore, getting chilled caused the cold even though medical experts tell us that the virus that causes colds must be communicated by another human being. Socrates and the other Greek orators did a lot of thinking about this kind of thinking and developed a whole system for analyzing the links between causes and their effects and when they are valid—that is, when such and such a cause did, in fact, bring about a particular effect—and spelled out ways to determine whether or not the reasoning is reliable. When it is not reliable, it is called a fallacy.

A common fallacy in reasoning is the *post hoc ergo propter hoc* ("after this, therefore because of this") or the false-cause fallacy. These errors occur in cause/effect reasoning, which may either go from cause to effect or effect to cause. They happen when an inadequate cause is offered for a particular effect; when the possibility of more than one cause is ignored; and when a connection between a particular cause and a particular effect is not made.

An example of a *post hoc*: Our sales shot up thirty-five percent after we ran that television campaign; therefore the campaign caused the increase in sales. It might have been a cause, of course, but more evidence is needed to prove it.

An example of an inadequate cause for a particular effect: An Iraqi truck driver reported that Saddam Hussein had nuclear weapons; therefore, Saddam Hussein is a threat to world security. More causes were needed to prove the conclusion.

An example of failing to make a connection between a particular cause and an effect assigned to it: Anna fell into a putrid pond on Saturday; on Monday she came down with polio; therefore, the polio was caused by the water in the pond. This, of course, is not acceptable unless the polio virus is found in a sample of water from the pond. A connection must be proven.

COMPETENCY 4.0   INTERPRETS TEXTUAL AND GRAPHIC
                 INFORMATION

Skill 4.1   Interprets information from tables, line graphs, bar graphs,
             and pie charts

Tables
To interpret data in tables, we read across rows and down columns. Each item of
interest has different data points listed under different column headings.

Table 1. Sample Purchase Order

Item	Unit	$/Unit	Qty	Total $
Coffee	Lb.	2.79	45	125.55
Milk	Gal.	1.05	72	75.60
Sugar	Lb.	0.23	150	34.50

In Table 1 (above), the first column on the left contains the items in a purchase
order. The other columns contain data about each item labeled with column
headings. The second column from the left gives the unit of measurement for
each item, the third column gives the price per unit, the fourth column gives the
quantity of each item ordered, and the fifth column gives the total cost of each
item.

Examples: Use Table 1 to answer the following questions.

             1. What does the 1.05 value in the table represent?

                Answer: Price in dollars per gallon of milk.

             2. What is the total cost of the purchase order?

                Answer: $235.65

             3. How many combined pounds of coffee and sugar does this
                purchase order purchase?

                Answer: 195 lbs.

See also Skill 15.3 for a description of how to create and interpret line graphs,
bar graphs and pie charts.

Quantitative data is often easily presented in graphs and charts in many content
areas. However, if students are unable to decipher the graph, their use becomes
limited to students. Since information can clearly be displayed in a graph or chart
form, accurate interpretation of the information is an important skill for students.

For graphs, students should be taught to evaluate all the features of the graph, including main title, what the horizontal axis represents and what the vertical axis represents. Also, students should locate and evaluate the graph's key (if there is one) in the event there is more than one variable on the graph. For example, line graphs are often used to plot data from a scientific experiment. If more than one variable were used, a key or legend would indicate what each line on the graph represented. Then, once students have evaluated the axes and titles, they can begin to assess the results of the experiment.

For charts (such as a pie chart), the process is similar to interpreting bar or line graphs. The key which depicts what each section of the pie chart represents is very important to interpreting the pie chart. Be sure to provide students with lots of assistance and practice with reading and interpreting graphs and charts so their experience with and confidence in reading them develops.

Skill 4.2 Recognizes appropriate representations of written information in graphic or tabular form

Many educational disciplines require the ability to recognize representations of written information in graphic or tabular form. Tables help condense and organize written data and graphs help reveal and emphasize comparisons and trends.

Example: A survey asked five elementary school students to list the number and type of pets they had at home. The first student had three dogs and three fish. The second student had two cats and one dog. The third student had three fish and two dogs. The fourth student had one rabbit, two cats, and one dog. The fifth student had no pets.

Construct a data table and line graph that represent the survey information.

Solution: The following is a table that appropriately represents the data.

Student #	# of Dogs	# of Cats	# of Fish	# of Rabbits	Total # of Pets
1	3	0	3	0	6
2	1	2	0	0	3
3	2	0	3	0	5
4	1	2	0	1	4
5	0	0	0	0	0

The following is a line graph that appropriately represents the total number of pets each student has.

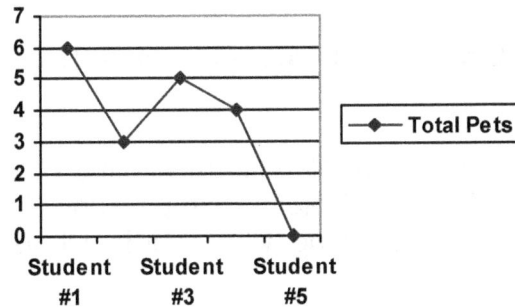

Skill 4.3   Recognizes differences between fact and opinion

A **fact** is something that is true and can be proved.

An **opinion** is something that a person believes, thinks, or feels.

Examine the following examples:

Joe DiMaggio, a Yankees' center-fielder, was replaced by Mickey Mantle in 1952.

This is a fact. If necessary, evidence can be produced to support this.

First year players are more ambitious than seasoned players.

This is an opinion. There is no proof to support that everyone feels this way.

SUBAREA II.   **WRITING**

COMPETENCY 5.0   UNDERSTANDS THE STANDARD USE OF VERBS

Skill 5.1   Identifies standard subject-verb agreement (e.g., number, person)

A verb must correspond in the singular or plural form with the simple subject; it is not affected by any interfering elements. Note: A simple subject is never found in a prepositional phrase (a phrase beginning with a word such as of, by, over, through, until).

Error: Sally, as well as her sister, plan to go into nursing.

Problem: The subject in the sentence is *Sally* alone, not the word *sister*. Therefore, the verb must be singular.

Correction: *Sally, as well as her sister, plans to go into nursing.*

Error: There has been many car accidents lately on that street.

Problem: The subject accidents in this sentence is plural; the verb must be plural also--even though it comes before the subject.

Correction: *There have been many car accidents lately on that street.*

Error: Everyone of us have a reason to attend the school musical.

Problem: The simple subject is the word *everyone*, not the *us* in the prepositional phrase. Therefore, the verb must be singular also.

Correction: *Everyone of us has a reason to attend the school musical.*

Error: Either the police captain or his officers is going to the convention.

Problem: In either/or and neither/nor constructions, the verb agrees with the subject closer to it.

Correction: *Either the police captain or his officers are going to the convention.*

Skill 5.2   Identifies verb tense (e.g., present, past)

Both regular and irregular verbs must appear in their standard forms for each tense. Note: the ed or d ending is added to regular verbs in the past tense and for past participles.

Error: She should have went to her doctor's appointment at the scheduled time.

Problem: The past participle of the verb *to go* is *gone*. *Went* expresses the simple past tense.

Correction: *She should have gone to her doctor's appointment at the scheduled time.*

Error: My train is suppose to arrive before two o'clock.

Problem: The verb following *train* is a present tense passive construction which requires the present tense verb *to be* and the past participle.

Correction: *My train is supposed to arrive before two o'clock.*

Error: Linda should of known that the car wouldn't start after leaving it out in the cold all night.

Problem: *Should of* is a nonstandard expression. *Of is* not a verb.

Correction: *Linda should have known that the car wouldn't start after leaving it out in the cold all night.*

Skill 5.3   Recognizes consistency of verb tense (e.g., verb endings)

Verb tenses must refer to the same time period consistently, unless a change in time is required.

Error: Despite the increased amount of students in the school this year, overall attendance is higher last year at the sporting events.

Problem: The verb *is* represents an inconsistent shift to the present tense when the action refers to a past occurrence.

Correction: *Despite the increased amount of students in the school this year, overall attendance was higher last year at sporting events.*

Error: My friend Lou, who just competed in the marathon, ran since he was twelve years old.

Problem: Because Lou continues to run, the present perfect tense is needed.

Correction: *My friend Lou, who just competed in the marathon, has run since he was twelve years old.*

Error: The Mayor congratulated Wallace Mangham, who renovates the city hall last year.

Problem: Although the speaker is talking in the present, the action of renovating the city hall was in the past.

Correction: *The Mayor congratulated Wallace Mangham, who renovated the city hall last year.*

COMPETENCY 6.0   UNDERSTANDS THE STANDARD USE OF PRONOUNS AND MODIFIERS

Skill 6.1   Identifies agreement (e.g., number, gender, person) between a pronoun and its antecedent

A **pronoun** is a word that replaces a noun or another pronoun. A pronoun must correspond with the singular or plural form of the noun, called the antecedent, to which it refers. Similarly, a pronoun must be in the same person (1st, 2nd, 3rd) as the noun. A pronoun must refer clearly to a single word, not to a complete idea.

Error: When an actor is rehearsing for a play, it often helps if you can memorize the lines in advance.

Problem: *Actor* is a third-person word; that is, the writer is talking about the subject. The pronoun *you* is in the second person, which means the writer is talking to the subject.

Correction: *When actors are rehearsing for plays, it helps if they can memorize the lines in advance.*

Error: The workers in the factory were upset when his or her paychecks didn't arrive on time.

Problem: *Workers* is a plural form, while *his or her* refers to one person.

Correction: *The workers in the factory were upset when their paychecks didn't arrive on time.*

Error: The charity auction was highly successful, which pleased everyone.

Problem: In this sentence the pronoun *which* refers to the idea of the auction's success. In fact, *which* has no antecedent in the sentence; the word success is not stated.

Correction: *Everyone was pleased at the success of the auction.*

Error: Lana told Melanie that she would like aerobics.

Problem: The person that she refers to is unclear; it could be either Lana or Melanie.

Correction: *Lana said that Melanie would like aerobics.*

OR

Lana told Melanie that she, Melanie, would like aerobics.

Error: I dislike accounting, even though my brother is one.

Problem: A person's occupation is not the same as a field, and the pronoun *one* is thus incorrect. Note that the word *accountant* is not used in the sentence, so *one* has no antecedent.

Correction: *I dislike accounting, even though my brother is an accountant.*

Skill 6.2   **Uses possessive pronouns (e.g., its vs. it's), relative pronouns (e.g., that, which), and demonstrative pronouns (e.g., this, that)**

Pronouns change case forms. Pronouns must be in the subjective, objective, or possessive case according to their function in the sentence.

Error: Tom and me have reserved seats for next week's baseball game.

Problem: The pronoun *me* is the subject of the verb *have reserved* and should be in the subjective form.

Correction: *Tom and I have reserved seats for next week's baseball game.*

Error: Mr. Green showed all of we students how to make paper hats.

Problem: The pronoun *we* is the object of the preposition *of*. It should be in the objective form, us.

Correction: *Mr. Green showed all of us students how to make paper hats.*

Possessive pronouns

Possessive pronouns indicate possession. Examples of possessive pronouns include *my, yours, his, hers, its, theirs,* and *whose*.

Error: Who's coat is this?

Problem: The interrogative possessive pronoun is whose; *who's* is the contraction for who is.

Correction: *Whose coat is this?*

Relative Pronouns

A relative pronoun relates to a noun preceding it in the sentence. Therefore, it connects a dependent clause to an antecedent (i.e., a noun that precedes the pronoun.) Therefore, the relative pronoun will act as the subject or object of the dependent clause. The relative pronouns are *who, whom, that,* and *which*. You can use relative pronouns to link a phrase or clause to another phrase or clause. Also, when referring to people use these relative pronouns *who* or *whoever* to refer to the subject of the clause, and you can use *whom* or *whomever* to refer to the objects of a verb or preposition.

Error: You may invite *whoever* to the graduation celebration.

Problem: The relative pronoun whoever in this sentence is not replacing the subject of the sentence, but the object to be invited.

Correction: *You may invite whomever to the graduation celebration.*

Error: The voters will choose the candidate whom has the best qualifications for the job.

Problem: The case of the relative pronoun who or whom is determined by the pronoun's function in the clause in which it appears. The word who is in the subjective case, and whom is in the objective. Analyze how the pronoun is being used within the sentence.

Correction: *The voters will choose the candidate who has the best qualifications for the job.*

These pronouns take a different case depending on whether the relative pronoun is a subject or an object in the dependent clause. Therefore, it becomes critical to not only know the subject and object forms of these pronouns but to be able to identify how they are being used in the dependent clause.

Who vs. Whom

When these relative pronouns are the subject (initiating the action) of the dependent clause, use the subjective case (*Who, Whoever*).

When these relative pronouns are the object (receiving the action) of the dependent clause, use the objective case (*Whom, Whomever*).

NOTE: *Who* and *whom* can be interrogative or personal pronouns rather than relative pronouns. In order to be a relative pronoun, it must refer to a noun preceding it.

Which vs. That

When referring to a place, thing or idea, use these relative pronouns (*Which, That*). When using relative pronouns for places, things or ideas, rather than determining case, you must decide whether the information in the dependent clause is essential to the meaning of the dependent clause or simply additional information. When information is critical to the understanding of the main clause, use *that* as the appropriate relative pronoun and do not set the information off by commas. The clause containing the pronoun and not set off by commas is referred to as a restrictive clause.

When information is NOT critical to the understanding of the main clause, use *which* as the appropriate relative pronoun and set the information off by commas. The clause set off by commas is referred to as a nonrestrictive dependent clause. Nonrestrictive relative pronouns describe, add incidental detail or begin new/separate ideas. There is usually a comma separating the non-restrictive clause from the main/independent clause.

Demonstrative Pronouns

A demonstrative pronoun points to and identifies a noun or a pronoun. *This* and *these* refer to things that are nearby either in space or in time, while *that* and *those* refer to things that are farther away in space or time. *This* and *that* are used to refer to singular nouns or noun phrases and *these* and *those* are used to refer to plural nouns and noun phrases.

Skill 6.3   Uses comparative and superlative modifiers (e.g., good/better/best)

A modifier can be an adjective, adverb, phrase or clause that provides more information to another element in the sentence.

Comparative Modifiers
Use the comparative form of an adjective or adverb to compare *exactly* two things. To form the comparative modifier, add the suffix "er" (such as *faster* or *smarter*) to the modifier (for some short words) or by using the word "more" with the modifier. *Better* is also a comparative modifier.

For example:
This pizza is *better* than that pizza.
Michelle was *quicker* to complete the problem than Sarah.
John sells *more* accounts than the rest of the team.

Superlative Modifiers
Use the superlative form to compare three or more things. To form the superlative modifier, add the suffix "est" (such as *tallest* or *biggest*) to the modifier (for some short words) or by using the word "most" with the modifier. *Best* is also a superlative modifier.

For example:
Carla has the *best* working attitude in her department.
In his class, Corey performed with the *most* confidence.
Jennifer has the *biggest* heart of all of my friends.

NOTE: When in doubt as to the appropriate form for the modifier, consult the dictionary. However, there are certain modifiers which you cannot logically use in the comparative and superlative forms. Adjectives like "perfect" and "unique," for instance, express absolute conditions and do not allow for degrees of comparison. Something cannot be *more* perfect than another thing: it is either perfect or not perfect.

COMPETENCY 7.0   UNDERSTANDS STANDARD SENTENCE STRUCTURE AND PUNCTUATION

Skill 7.1   Distinguishes between sentence fragments and complete sentences

Fragments occur (1) if word groups standing alone are missing either a subject or a verb, and (2) if word groups containing a subject and verb and standing alone are actually made dependent because of the use of subordinating conjunctions or relative pronouns.

Error: The teacher waiting for the class to complete the assignment.

Problem: This sentence is not complete because an "*ing*" word alone does not function as a verb. When a helping verb is added (for example, was waiting), it will become a sentence.

Correction: *The teacher was waiting for the class to complete the assignment.*

Error: Until the last toy was removed from the floor.

Problem: Words such as until, because, although, when, and if make a clause dependent and thus incapable of standing alone. An independent clause must be added to make the sentence complete.

Correction: *Until the last toy was removed from the floor, the kids could not go outside to play.*

Error: The city will close the public library. Because of a shortage of funds.

Problem: The problem is the same as above. The dependent clause must be joined to the independent clause.

Correction: *The city will close the public library because of a shortage of funds.*

Error: Anyone planning to go on the trip should bring the necessary items. Such as a backpack, boots, a canteen, and bug spray.

Problem: The second word group is a phrase and cannot stand alone because there is neither a subject nor a verb. The fragment can be corrected by adding the phrase to the sentence.

Correction: *Anyone planning to go on the trip should bring the necessary items, such as a backpack, boots, a canteen, and bug spray.*

Skill 7.2   **Distinguishes between run-on sentences and correctly divided sentences**

A run-on sentence consists of two or more independent clauses that have been joined together without a conjunction or the correct punctuation. A run-on sentence will contain two or more independent clauses. Two subjects within the same sentence (or a subject and a pronoun) may indicate a run-on sentence. Run-on sentences can be converted to correctly divided sentences as follows:

- separate the independent clauses/sentences using periods
- add a comma and a conjunction such as and, but, or, so, yet
- place a semicolon between the independent clauses
- change one of the sentences into a clause beginning with because

Review the following run-on sentences, consider how you would correct them and then review the sample corrections.

Examples of run-on sentences
1) He is my best friend he looks after me and takes good care of me.
2) She sleeps all day she studies and writes all night.
3) I'm not sure how she will make out it isn't easy working all night.
4) Of course he likes the idea even so he's unlikely to take on the responsibility unless he's asked to do so.

Corrections
1) He is my best friend. He looks after me and takes good care of me.
2) She sleeps all day because she studies and writes all night.
3) I'm not sure how she will make out; it isn't easy working all night.
4) Of course he likes the idea, but even so, he's unlikely to take on the responsibility unless he's asked to do so.

Skill 7.3   Identifies correct and incorrect punctuation

Commas
Commas indicate a brief pause. They are used to set off dependent clauses and long introductory word groups. They are also used to separate words in a series. They are used to set off unimportant material that interrupts the flow of the sentence, and they separate independent clauses joined by conjunctions.

Error: After I finish my master's thesis I plan to work in Chicago.

Problem: A comma is needed after an introductory dependent word-group containing a subject and verb.

Correction: *After I finish my master's thesis, I plan to work in Chicago.*

Error: I washed waxed and vacuumed my car today.

Problem: Words in a series should be separated by commas. Although the word *and* is sometimes considered optional, it is often necessary to clarify the meaning.

Correction: *I washed, waxed, and vacuumed my car today.*

Error: She was a talented dancer but she is mostly remembered for her singing ability.

Problem: A comma is needed before a conjunction that joins two independent clauses (complete sentences).

Correction: *She was a talented dancer, but she is mostly remembered for her singing ability.*

Error: This incident is I think typical of what can happen when the community remains so divided.

Problem: Commas are needed between nonessential words or words that interrupt the main clause.

Correction: *This incident is, I think, typical of what can happen when the community remains so divided.*

Semicolons and colons

Semicolons are needed to divide two or more closely related independent sentences. They are also needed to separate items in a series containing commas. Colons are used to introduce lists and to emphasize what follows.

Error: I climbed to the top of the mountain, it took me three hours.

Problem: A comma alone cannot separate two independent clauses. Instead a semicolon is needed to separate two related sentences.

Correction: *I climbed to the top of the mountain; it took me three hours.*

Error: In the movie, asteroids destroyed Dallas, Texas, Kansas City, Missouri, and Boston, Massachusetts.

Problem: Semicolons are needed to separate items in a series that already contains commas.

Correction: *In the movie, asteroids destroyed Dallas, Texas; Kansas City, Missouri; and Boston, Massachusetts.*

Error: Essays will receive the following grades, A for excellent, B for good, C for average, and D for unsatisfactory.

Problem: A colon is needed to emphasize the information or list that follows.

Correction: *Essays will receive the following grades: A for excellent, B for good, C for average, and D for unsatisfactory.*

Error: The school carnival included: amusement rides, clowns, food booths, and a variety of games.

Problem: The material preceding the colon and the list that follows is not a complete sentence. Do not separate a verb (or preposition) from the object.

Correction: *The school carnival included amusement rides, clowns, food booths, and a variety of games.*

Apostrophes

Apostrophes are used to show either contractions or possession.

Error: She shouldnt be permitted to smoke cigarettes in the building.

Problem: An apostrophe is needed in a contraction in place of the missing letter.

Correction: *She shouldn't be permitted to smoke cigarettes in the building.*

Error: My cousins motorcycle was stolen from his driveway.

Problem: An apostrophe is needed to show possession.

Correction: *My cousin's motorcycle was stolen from his driveway.*
(Note: The use of the apostrophe before the letter "s" means that there is just one cousin. The plural form would read the following way: My cousins' motorcycle was stolen from their driveway.)

Error: The childrens new kindergarten teacher was also a singer.

Problem: An apostrophe is needed to show possession.

Correction: *The childrens' new kindergarten teacher was also a singer.*
(Note: The apostrophe after the "s" indicates that there is more than one child).

Error: Children screams could be heard for miles.

Problem: An apostrophe and the letter s are needed in the sentence to show whose screams it is.

Correction: *Children's screams could be heard for miles.*
(Note: Because the word children is already plural, the apostrophe and s must be added afterward to show ownership.)

Quotation marks

Use double quotation marks to enclose a direct quotation and to enclose the title of an article, a song, an essay, or a short story.

Error:　　Franklin Roosevelt once said, There is nothing to fear but fear itself.

Problem:　　Double quotation marks are needed to set off the quotation.

Correction:　*Franklin Roosevelt once said, "There is nothing to fear but fear itself."*

Correction:　*In his article, "How to Fish for Trout," Leonard gives good advice to the beginning fisherman.*

Error:　　In the song Streets of Philadelphia, Bruce Springsteen pays tribute to a man dying from AIDS.

Problem:　　Use double quotations to set off the title of a song.

Correction:　*In the song "Streets of Philadelphia," Bruce Springsteen pays tribute to a man dying from AIDS.*

COMPETENCY 8.0   UNDERSTANDS THE STANDARD USE OF CAPITALIZATION AND SPELLING

Skill 8.1   Identifies standard capitalization at the beginning of sentences

Capital letters are used to indicate specific names of people, places, buildings, companies, courses, products, holidays, days of the week, months, and major sections of the country and the world. Capital letters are also used to signal the start of a sentence and of a direct quotation.

Error: Emma went to Dr. Peters for treatment since her own Doctor was on vacation.

Problem: The use of capital letters with Emma and Dr .Peters is correct since they are specific (proper) names; the title Dr. is also capitalized. However, the word doctor is not a specific name and should not be capitalized.

Correction: *Emma went to Dr. Peters for treatment since her own doctor was on vacation.*

Error: Our Winter Break does not start until next wednesday.

Problem: Days of the week are capitalized, but seasons are not capitalized.

Correction: *Our winter break does not start until next Wednesday.*

Error: The exchange student from israel who came to study biochemistry spoke spanish very well.

Problem: Languages and the names of countries are always capitalized. Courses are also capitalized when they refer to a specific course; they are not capitalized when they refer to courses in general.

Correction: *The exchange student from Israel who came to study Biochemistry spoke Spanish very well.*

Skill 8.2   Identifies standard capitalization of proper words and titles

See Skill 8.1

Skill 8.3   Recognizes standard spelling of commonly encountered words presented in context

Spelling correctly is not always easy because English not only utilizes an often inconsistent spelling system, but also uses many words derived from other languages. Good spelling is important because incorrect spelling damages the physical appearance of writing and may puzzle your reader.

The following is a list of commonly misspelled words:

1. commitment	21. possession
2. succeed	22. accumulate
3. necessary	23. hospitality
4. connected	24. judgment
5. opportunity	25. conscious
6. embarrassed	26. height
7. occasionally	27. leisurely
8. receive	28. shield
9. their	29. foreign
10. accelerate	30. innovative
11. patience	31. similar
12. obstinate	32. proceed
13. achievement	33. contemporary
14. responsibility	34. beneficial
15. prejudice	35. attachment
16. familiar	36. guarantee
17. hindrance	37. tropical
18. controversial	38. misfortune
19. publicity	39. particular
20. prescription	40. yield

I BEFORE E

i before e	grieve, fiend, niece, friend
except after c	receive, conceive, receipt
or when sounded like "a"	as in reindeer and weight, and reign
Exceptions:	weird, foreign, seize, leisure

As students acquire and develop spelling skills, they should readily be able to recognize commonly encountered words when presented in context. The practice of recognizing new spelling/study words when presented in context will serve as an aid to improving spelling, pronunciation and understanding of words for most students.

In the sample, below, it is easy to see how the use of spelling/study words in context illustrates any similarities, differences or nuances and may help the student determine the appropriate choice and correct spelling of words.

Sample of Spelling Words within Context

There	Their	They're
Are	Hour	Our
Week	Weak	
Its	It's	
Knight	Night	
Eight	Ate	

We stayed in a very old house in England, during <u>our</u> vacation. It belonged to <u>our</u> friends. <u>They're</u> fortunate to own a manor house. We were <u>there</u> for <u>eight</u> days. <u>There</u> <u>are</u> many interesting things in the house. <u>Their</u> prized possession is a suit of armor which was once worn by a <u>knight</u>. <u>Its</u> helmet had a hinged part that could open or close over the face. We went on a tour of the countryside. <u>It's</u> so beautiful! But we were away for almost <u>eight</u> <u>hours</u>. It was late at <u>night</u> when we got back. I was <u>weak</u> from hunger. I <u>ate</u> enough dinner for two people. Next year, I'm going back to visit for another <u>week</u>.

SUBAREA III.   **MATHEMATICS**

COMPETENCY 9.0   UNDERSTANDS NUMBER CONCEPTS

Skill 9.1   **Identifies the place value of digits (e.g., hundreds, tens, ones, tenths)**

Whole Number Place Value

Consider the number 792. We can assign a place value to each digit.

Reading from left to right, the first digit (7) represents the hundreds' place. The hundreds' place tells us how many sets of one hundred the number contains. Thus, there are 7 sets of one hundred in the number 792.

The second digit (9) represents the tens' place. The tens' place tells us how many sets of ten the number contains. Thus, there are 9 sets of ten in the number 792.

The last digit (2) represents the ones' place. The ones' place tells us how many ones the number contains. Thus, there are 2 sets of one in the number 792.

Therefore, there are 7 sets of 100, plus 9 sets of 10, plus 2 ones in the number 792.

Decimal Place Value

More complex numbers have additional place values to both the left and right of the decimal point. Consider the number 374.8.

Reading from left to right, the first digit (3) is in the hundreds' place and tells us the number contains 3 sets of one hundred.

The second digit (7) is in the tens' place and tells us the number contains 7 sets of ten.

The third digit (4) is in the ones' place and tells us the number contains 4 ones.

Finally, the number after the decimal (8) is in the tenths' place and tells us the number contains 8 tenths.

Skill 9.2   Identifies correctly rounded numbers (e.g., to the nearest ten)

Rounding numbers is a form of estimation that is very useful in many mathematical operations. For example, when estimating the sum of two three-digit numbers, it is helpful to round the two numbers to the nearest hundred prior to addition. We can round numbers to any place value.

Rounding whole numbers

To round whole numbers, you first find the place value you want to round to (the rounding digit) and look at the digit directly to the right. If the digit is less than five, do not change the rounding digit and replace all numbers after the rounding digit with zeroes. If the digit is greater than or equal to five, increase the rounding digit by one and replace all numbers after the rounding digit with zeroes.

Example: Round 517 to the nearest ten.

1 is the rounding digit because it occupies the tens' place.

517 rounded to the nearest ten = 520; because 7 > 5 we add one to the rounding digit.

Example: Round 15,449 to the nearest hundred.

The first 4 is the rounding digit because it occupies the hundreds' place.

15,449 rounded to the nearest hundred = 15,400, because 4 < 5 we do not add to the rounding digit.

Rounding decimals

Rounding decimals is identical to rounding whole numbers except that you simply drop all the digits to the right of the rounding digit.

Example: Round 417.3621 to the nearest tenth.

3 is the rounding digit because it occupies the tenth place.

417.3621 rounded to the nearest tenth = 417.4; because 6 > 5 we add one to the rounding digit.

Skill 9.3   **Identifies equivalent weights and measures in different units (e.g., feet and inches, quarts and pints, kilograms and grams)**

<u>Measurements of length (English system)</u>

12 inches (in)	=	1 foot (ft)
3 feet (ft)	=	1 yard (yd)
1760 yards (yd)	=	1 mile (mi)

<u>Measurements of length (Metric system)</u>

1 kilometer (km)	=	1000 meters (m)
1 hectometer (hm)	=	100 meters (m)
1 decameter (dam)	=	10 meters (m)
1 meter (m)	=	1 meter (m)
1 decimeter (dm)	=	1/10 meter (m)
1 centimeter (cm)	=	1/100 meter (m)
1 millimeter (mm)	=	1/1000 meter (m)

<u>Conversion of length from English to Metric</u>

1 inch	=	2.54 centimeters
1 foot	≈	30 centimeters
1 yard	≈	0.9 meters
1 mile	≈	1.6 kilometers

<u>Measurements of weight (English system)</u>

28 grams (g)	=	1 ounce (oz)
16 ounces (oz)	=	1 pound (lb)
2000 pounds (lb)	=	1 ton (t)

<u>Measurements of weight (Metric system)</u>

1 kilogram (kg)	=	1000 grams (g)
1 gram (g)	=	1 gram (g)
1 milligram (mg)	=	1/1000 gram (g)

<u>Conversion of weight from English to Metric</u>

1 ounce	≈	28 grams
1 pound	≈	0.45 kilograms
	≈	454 grams

Measurement of volume (English system)

8 fluid ounces (oz)	=	1 cup (c)
2 cups (c)	=	1 pint (pt)
2 pints (pt)	=	1 quart (qt)
4 quarts (qt)	=	1 gallon (gal)

Measurement of volume (Metric system)

1 kiloliter (kl)	=	1000 liters (l)
1 liter (l)	=	1 liter (l)
1 milliliter (ml)	=	1/1000 liters (ml)

Conversion of volume from English to Metric

1 teaspoon (tsp)	$\approx$	5 milliliters
1 fluid ounce	$\approx$	15 milliliters
1 cup	$\approx$	0.24 liters
1 pint	$\approx$	0.47 liters
1 quart	$\approx$	0.95 liters
1 gallon	$\approx$	3.8 liters

Measurement of time

1 minute	=	60 seconds
1 hour	=	60 minutes
1 day	=	24 hours
1 week	=	7 days
1 year	=	365 days
1 century	=	100 years

Note: (') represents feet and (") represents inches.

Skill 9.4 **Estimates the solution to a measurement problem (e.g., height, distance, perimeter)**

To estimate measurement of familiar objects, it is first necessary to determine the units to use.

Examples:
Length
1. The coastline of Florida
2. The width of a ribbon
3. The thickness of a book
4. The depth of water in a pool

Weight or mass
1. A bag of sugar
2. A school bus
3. A dime

Capacity or volume
1. Paint in a paint can
2. Glass of milk

Money
1. Cost of a house
2. Cost of a cup of coffee
3. Exchange rate

Perimeter
1. The edge of a backyard
2. The edge of a football field
Area
1. The size of a carpet
2. The size of a state

Example: Estimate the measurements of the following objects:

Length of a dollar bill	6 inches
Weight of a baseball	1 pound
Distance from New York to Florida	1100 km
Volume of water to fill a medicine dropper	1 milliliter
Length of a desk	2 meters
Temperature of water in a swimming pool	80° F

Depending on the degree of accuracy needed, we can measure an object with different units. For example, a pencil may be 6 inches to the nearest inch or 6 3/8 inches to the nearest eighth of an inch. Similarly, it might be 15 cm to the nearest cm or 154 mm to the nearest mm.

Given a set of objects and their measurements, the use of rounding procedures is helpful when attempting to round to the nearest given unit. When rounding to a given place value, it is necessary to look at the number in the next smaller place. If this number is 5 or more, we increase the number in the place we are rounding and change all numbers to the right to zero. If the number is less than 5, the we leave the number in the place we are rounding the same and change all numbers to the right to zero.

One method of rounding measurements can require an additional step. First, we must convert the measurement to a decimal number. Then, we apply the rules for rounding.

Example: Round the measurements to the given units.

MEASUREMENT	ROUND TO NEAREST	ANSWER
1 foot 7 inches	foot	2 ft
5 pound 6 ounces	pound	5 pounds
5 9/16 inches	inch	6 inches

Convert each measurement to a decimal number, then apply the rules for rounding.

1 foot 7 inches = $1\frac{7}{12}$ ft = 1.58333 ft, round up to 2 ft

5 pounds 6 ounces = $5\frac{6}{16}$ pounds = 5.375 pound, round to 5 pounds

$5\frac{9}{16}$ inches = 5.5625 inches, round up to 6 inches

Estimating Height – The most effective method of estimating height is to compare the height of an object to an object of known height. For example, a student can estimate the height of other students by comparing his height to the height of the other students. To estimate the height of large objects (e.g. trees, buildings), we can take a picture of the object with an object of known height next to it. Then we can use a ruler to estimate the height of the large object by comparison.

Estimating Distance – An effective method of estimating short distances is "stepping off" or "pacing". Walking the distance and counting the number of steps allows us to estimate the distance in yards or meters. An effective method of estimating longer distances is to use objects as points of comparison. For example, we can estimate distance outdoors by noting the apparent size of trees or buildings at our current location and our destination.

Estimating Perimeter – We can estimate the perimeter of geometric shapes by estimating the length of one portion of the shape (e.g. side of a polygon). For example, we can estimate that the perimeter of an octagon with sides measuring approximately one inch is eight inches. We can also estimate the perimeter of large objects, like pieces of property or lakes, by extrapolating from basic measurements. For example, to estimate the perimeter of a lake with a ragged, curved perimeter, we would take straight-line measurements around the edge of the lake and add them together.

COMPETENCY 10.0 UNDERSTANDS THE ADDITION AND SUBTRACTION OF WHOLE NUMBERS

Skill 10.1 Solves problems involving the addition of whole numbers

Addition is one of the four basic number operations. Addition involves the combining of two values or quantities. We call the answer of an addition problem a sum.

The basic algorithm of addition involves aligning numbers by place value and adding each place value column. When a column totals more than ten, we "carry" the tens' digit of the sum to the next column and add it there.

Example: At the end of a day of shopping, a shopper had $24 remaining in his wallet. He spent $45 on various goods. How much money did the shopper have at the beginning of the day?

The total amount of money the shopper started with is the sum of the amount spent and the amount remaining at the end of the day.

$$\begin{array}{r} 24 \\ + \ 45 \\ \hline 69 \end{array}$$ → The original total was $69.

Example: The winner of a race took 1 hr. 58 min. 12 sec. on the first half of the race and 2 hr. 9 min. 57 sec. on the second half of the race. What was the winner's total time?

1 hr. 58 min. 12 sec.
+ 2 hr. 9 min. 57 sec.   Add these numbers
3 hr. 67 min. 69 sec.
+   1 min - 60 sec.   Change 60 seconds to 1min.
3 hr. 68 min. 9 sec.
+ 1 hr.-60 min.   .   Change 60 minutes to 1 hr.
4 hr. 8 min. 9 sec. ← Final answer

Example: A biology student counts the number of oranges on three orange trees. The student counted 103 oranges on the first tree, 85 on the second tree, and 122 on the third tree. How many total oranges do the trees contain?

The total number of oranges is the sum of the counts of the three trees.
(1)(1)
103
85   → Note the that we had to carry a one
+ 122   to both the tens' column and the
310 oranges   hundreds' column.

Skill 10.2   Solves problems involving the subtraction of whole numbers

Subtraction is another of the four basic number operations. Subtraction involves taking a quantity or value away from another quantity or value. We call the answer to a subtraction problem the difference.

The basic algorithm for subtraction is the similar to the algorithm for addition. We align the numbers by place value and subtract each column. If the number in the top column is smaller than the number below it, we "borrow" a ten from the tens' column and add it to the top number.

Example: Find the difference of 57 and 39.

$$\begin{array}{c} 57 \\ -\ 39 \end{array} \longrightarrow \begin{array}{c} 57 \\ -\ 39 \end{array} \longrightarrow \begin{array}{c} (5\text{-}1=4),\ (7+10=17) \\ 4(17) \\ -\ 39 \\ \hline 18 \end{array}$$

Note that because 7 is less than 9 we borrow a ten from the 5 in the tens' column. This leaves a 4 and adding ten to the 7 produces 17. Thus, $17 - 9 = 8$ and $4 - 3 = 1$. The final difference is 18.

Example: At the end of his shift, a cashier has $96 in the cash register. At the beginning of his shift, he had $15. How much money did the cashier collect during his shift?

The total collected is the difference of the ending amount and the starting amount.

$$\begin{array}{c} 96 \\ -\ 15 \\ \hline 81 \end{array} \longrightarrow \text{The total collected was \$81.}$$

Skill 10.3   Applies principles of addition and subtraction of whole numbers to solve problems encountered in everyday life

See Skills 10.1 and 10.2.

COMPETENCY 11.0   UNDERSTANDS MULTIPLICATION AND DIVISION OF WHOLE NUMBERS

Skill 11.1 Solves problems involving the multiplication of whole numbers

Multiplication is one of the four basic number operations. In simple terms, multiplication is the addition of a number to itself a certain number of times. For example, 4 multiplied by 3 is the equal to 4 + 4 + 4 or 3 + 3 + 3 +3. Another way of conceptualizing multiplication is to think in terms of groups. For example, if we have 4 groups of 3 students, the total number of students is 4 multiplied by 3. We call the solution to a multiplication problem the product.

The basic algorithm for whole number multiplication begins with aligning the numbers by place value with the number containing more places on top.

$$
\begin{array}{r}
172 \\
\times\ \ 43 \\
\end{array}
\longrightarrow
$$
Note that we placed 122 on top because it has more places than 43 does.

Next, we multiply the ones' place of the second number by each place value of the top number sequentially.

$$
\begin{array}{r}
(2) \\
172 \\
\times\ \ 43 \\
\hline
516 \\
\end{array}
\longrightarrow
$$
{3 x 2 = 6, 3 x 7 = 21, 3 x 1 = 3}
Note that we had to carry a 2 to the hundreds' column because 3 x 7 = 21. Note also that we add, not multiply, carried numbers to the product.

Next, we multiply the number in the tens' place of the second number by each place value of the top number sequentially. Because we are multiplying by a number in the tens' place, we place a zero at the end of this product.

$$
\begin{array}{r}
(2) \\
172 \\
\times\ \ 43 \\
\hline
516 \\
6880 \\
\end{array}
\longrightarrow
$$
{4 x 2 = 8, 4 x 7 = 28, 4 x 1 = 4}

Finally, to determine the final product we add the two partial products.

$$
\begin{array}{r}
172 \\
\times\ \ 43 \\
\hline
516 \\
+\ 6880 \\
\hline
7396 \\
\end{array}
\longrightarrow
$$
The product of 172 and 43 is 7396.

Example: A student buys 4 boxes of crayons. Each box contains 16 crayons. How many total crayons does the student have?

The total number of crayons is 16 x 4.

$$
\begin{array}{r}
16 \\
\times\ 4 \\
\hline
64
\end{array}
$$
→ Total number of crayons equals 64.

Skill 11.2   Solves problems involving the division of whole numbers

Division, the inverse of multiplication, is another of the four basic number operations. When we divide one number by another, we determine how many times we can multiply the divisor (number divided by) before we exceed the number we are dividing (dividend). For example, 8 divided by 2 equals 4 because we can multiply 2 four times to reach 8 (2 x 4 = 8 or 2 + 2 + 2 + 2 = 8). Using the grouping conceptualization we used with multiplication, we can divide 8 into 4 groups of 2 or 2 groups of 4. We call the answer to a division problem the quotient.

If the divisor does not divide evenly into the dividend, we express the leftover amount either as a remainder or as a fraction with the divisor as the denominator. For example, 9 divided by 2 equals 4 with a remainder of 1 or 4 ½.

The basic algorithm for division is long division. We start by representing the quotient as follows.

$14\overline{)293}$ → 14 is the divisor and 293 is the dividend.

This represents 293 ÷ 14.

Next, we divide the divisor into the dividend starting from the left.

$14\overline{)293}^{2}$ → 14 divides into 29 two times with a remainder.

Next, we multiply the partial quotient by the divisor, subtract this value from the first digits of the dividend, and bring down the remaining dividend digits to complete the number.

13.

$$
\begin{array}{r}
2 \\
14\overline{)293} \\
-28 \\
\hline
13
\end{array}
$$
→ 2 x 14 = 28, 29 – 28 = 1, and bringing down the 3 yields

Finally, we divide again (the divisor into the remaining value) and repeat the preceding process. The number left after the subtraction represents the remainder.

$$
\begin{array}{r}
20 \\
14\overline{)293} \\
-28 \\
\hline
13 \\
-0 \\
\hline
13
\end{array}
$$

The final quotient is 20 with a remainder of 13. We can also represent this quotient as 20 13/14.

Example: Each box of apples contains 24 apples. How many boxes must a grocer purchase to supply a group of 252 people with one apple each?

The grocer needs 252 apples. Because he must buy apples in groups of 24, we divide 252 by 24 to determine how many boxes he needs to buy.

$$
\begin{array}{r}
10 \\
24\overline{)252} \\
-24 \\
\hline
12 \\
-0 \\
\hline
12
\end{array}
$$

The quotient is 10 with a remainder of 12.

Thus, the grocer needs 10 boxes plus 12 more apples. Therefore, the minimum number of boxes the grocer can purchase is 11.

Example: At his job, John gets paid $20 for every hour he works. If John made $940 in a week, how many hours did he work?

This is a division problem. To determine the number of hours John worked, we divide the total amount made ($940) by the hourly rate of pay ($20). Thus, the number of hours worked equals 940 divided by 20.

$$
\begin{array}{r}
47 \\
20{\overline{\smash{\big)}\,940}} \\
\underline{-80} \\
140 \\
\underline{-140} \\
0
\end{array}
$$

→ 20 divides into 940, 47 times with no remainder.

John worked 47 hours.

Skill 11.3   Applies principles of multiplication and division of whole numbers to solve problems encountered in everyday life

See Skills 11.1 and 11.2.

COMPETENCY 12.0 UNDERSTANDS OPERATIONS INVOLVING FRACTIONS, DECIMALS AND PERCENTS

Skill 12.1 Solves problems involving fractions (e.g., recipes)

A fraction is a part of a whole number. The denominator (bottom number of a fraction) tells us how many parts we are dividing the whole into and the numerator (top number of a fraction) tells us how many whole parts we are dealing with.

Addition and subtraction of fractions

<u>Key Points</u>

1. You need a common denominator in order to add and subtract reduced and improper fractions.

   Example: $\dfrac{1}{3} + \dfrac{7}{3} = \dfrac{1+7}{3} = \dfrac{8}{3} = 2\dfrac{2}{3}$

   Example: $\dfrac{4}{12} + \dfrac{6}{12} - \dfrac{3}{12} = \dfrac{4+6-3}{12} = \dfrac{7}{12}$

2. Adding an integer and a fraction of the <u>same</u> sign results directly in a mixed fraction.

   Example: $2 + \dfrac{2}{3} = 2\dfrac{2}{3}$

   Example: $^{-}2 - \dfrac{3}{4} = ^{-}2\dfrac{3}{4}$

3. Adding an integer and a fraction with different signs involves the following steps.

   -get a common denominator
   -add or subtract as needed
   -change to a mixed fraction if possible

   Example: $2 - \dfrac{1}{3} = \dfrac{2 \times 3 - 1}{3} = \dfrac{6-1}{3} = \dfrac{5}{3} = 1\dfrac{2}{3}$

Example: Add $7\dfrac{3}{8} + 5\dfrac{2}{7}$

Add the whole numbers; add the fractions and combine the two results:

$$7\dfrac{3}{8} + 5\dfrac{2}{7} = (7+5) + (\dfrac{3}{8} + \dfrac{2}{7})$$

$$= 12 + \dfrac{(7 \times 3) + (8 \times 2)}{56} \quad \text{(LCM of 8 and 7)}$$

$$= 12 + \dfrac{21 + 16}{56} = 12 + \dfrac{37}{56} = 12\dfrac{37}{56}$$

Example: Perform the operation.

$$\dfrac{2}{3} - \dfrac{5}{6}$$

We first find the LCM of 3 and 6 which is 6.

$$\dfrac{2 \times 2}{3 \times 2} - \dfrac{5}{6} \rightarrow \dfrac{4-5}{6} = \dfrac{^-1}{6} \quad \text{(Using method A)}$$

Example: $^-7\dfrac{1}{4} + 2\dfrac{7}{8}$

$$^-7\dfrac{1}{4} + 2\dfrac{7}{8} = (^-7 + 2) + (\dfrac{^-1}{4} + \dfrac{7}{8})$$

$$= (^-5) + \dfrac{(^-2 + 7)}{8} = (^-5) + (\dfrac{5}{8})$$

$$= (^-5) + \dfrac{5}{8} = \dfrac{^-5 \times 8}{1 \times 8} + \dfrac{5}{8} = \dfrac{^-40 + 5}{8}$$

$$= \dfrac{^-35}{8} = ^-4\dfrac{3}{8}$$

Divide 35 by 8 to get 4, remainder 3.

Caution: Common error would be

$$^-7\frac{1}{4}+2\frac{7}{8}=^-7\frac{2}{8}+2\frac{7}{8}=^-5\frac{9}{8}$$ Wrong.

It is correct to add -7 and 2 to get -5, but adding $\dfrac{2}{8}+\dfrac{7}{8}=\dfrac{9}{8}$

is wrong. It should have been $\dfrac{^-2}{8}+\dfrac{7}{8}=\dfrac{5}{8}$. Then,

$$^-5+\frac{5}{8}=^-4\frac{3}{8}$$ as before.

Multiplication of fractions

Using the following example: $3\dfrac{1}{4}\times\dfrac{5}{6}$

1. Convert each number to an improper fraction.

$$3\frac{1}{4}=\frac{(12+1)}{4}=\frac{13}{4}$$ $\dfrac{5}{6}$ is already in reduced form.

2. Reduce (cancel) common factors of the numerator and denominator if they exist.

$$\frac{13}{4}\times\frac{5}{6}$$ No common factors exist.

3. Multiply the numerators by each other and the denominators by each other.

$$\frac{13}{4}\times\frac{5}{6}=\frac{65}{24}$$

4. If possible, reduce the fraction back to its lowest term.

$$\frac{65}{24}$$ Cannot be reduced further.

5. Convert the improper fraction back to a mixed fraction by using long division.

$$\frac{65}{24}=24\overline{)65} \quad =2\frac{17}{24}$$
$$\phantom{\frac{65}{24}=24)}\underline{48}$$
$$\phantom{\frac{65}{24}=24)}17$$

Summary of sign changes for multiplication:

a. $(+) \times (+) = (+)$

b. $(-) \times (+) = (-)$

c. $(+) \times (-) = (-)$

d. $(-) \times (-) = (+)$

Example: $7\frac{1}{3} \times \frac{5}{11} = \frac{22}{3} \times \frac{5}{11}$ Reduce like terms (22 and 11)

$$= \frac{2}{3} \times \frac{5}{1} = \frac{10}{3} = 3\frac{1}{3}$$

Example: $^-6\frac{1}{4} \times \frac{5}{9} = \frac{^-25}{4} \times \frac{5}{9}$

$$= \frac{^-125}{36} = ^- 3\frac{17}{36}$$

Example: $\frac{^-1}{4} \times \frac{^-3}{7}$ Negative times a negative equals positive.

$$= \frac{1}{4} \times \frac{3}{7} = \frac{3}{28}$$

Division of fractions:

1. Change mixed fractions to improper fraction.

2. Change the division problem to a multiplication problem by using the reciprocal of the number after the division sign.

3. Find the sign of the final product.

4. Cancel if common factors exist between the numerator and the denominator.

5. Multiply the numerators together and the denominators together.

6. Change the improper fraction to a mixed number.

Example: $3\dfrac{1}{5} \div 2\dfrac{1}{4} = \dfrac{16}{5} \div \dfrac{9}{4}$

$= \dfrac{16}{5} \times \dfrac{4}{9}$ Reciprocal of $\dfrac{9}{4}$ is $\dfrac{4}{9}$.

$= \dfrac{64}{45} = 1\dfrac{19}{45}$

Example: $7\dfrac{3}{4} \div 11\dfrac{5}{8} = \dfrac{31}{4} \div \dfrac{93}{8}$

$= \dfrac{31}{4} \times \dfrac{8}{93}$ Reduce like terms.

$= \dfrac{1}{1} \times \dfrac{2}{3} = \dfrac{2}{3}$

Example: $\left(^-2\dfrac{1}{2}\right) \div 4\dfrac{1}{6} = \dfrac{^-5}{2} \div \dfrac{25}{6}$

$= \dfrac{^-5}{2} \times \dfrac{6}{25}$ Reduce like terms.

$= \dfrac{^-1}{1} \times \dfrac{3}{5} = \dfrac{^-3}{5}$

Example: $\left(^-5\dfrac{3}{8}\right) \div \left(\dfrac{^-7}{16}\right) = \dfrac{^-43}{8} \div \dfrac{^-7}{16}$

$= \dfrac{^-43}{8} \times \dfrac{^-16}{7}$ Reduce like terms.

$= \dfrac{43}{1} \times \dfrac{2}{7}$ Negative times a negative equals a positive.

$= \dfrac{86}{7} = 12\dfrac{2}{7}$

Skill 12.2   Solves problems involving decimals (e.g., money)

When we complete the division of fractions, we produce decimal numbers. For example, we can express the fraction ½ as 0.5. Operations with decimals are similar to whole numbers with a few key differences.

Addition and Subtraction of Decimals

When adding and subtracting decimals, we align the numbers by place value as we do with whole numbers. After adding or subtracting each column, we bring the decimal down, placing it in the same location as in the numbers added or subtracted.

Example: Find the sum of 152.3 and 36.342.

$$
\begin{array}{r}
152.300 \\
+\ \ 36.342 \\
\hline
188.642
\end{array}
$$

Note that we placed two zeroes after the final place value in 152.3 to clarify the column addition.

Example: Find the difference of 152.3 and 36.342.

$$
\begin{array}{r}
2\ 9\ 10 \\
152.\cancel{300} \\
-\ \ 36.342 \\
\hline
58
\end{array}
\longrightarrow
\begin{array}{r}
(4)11(12) \\
152.\cancel{300} \\
-\ \ 36.342 \\
\hline
115.958
\end{array}
$$

Note how we borrowed to subtract from the zeroes in the hundredths' and thousandths' place of 152.300.

Multiplication of Decimals

When multiplying decimal numbers, we multiply exactly as with whole numbers and place the decimal moving in from the left the total number of decimal places contained in the two numbers multiplied. For example, when multiplying 1.5 and 2.35, we place the decimal in the product 3 places in from the left (3.525).

Example: Find the product of 3.52 and 4.1.

$$
\begin{array}{r}
3.52 \\
\times\ \ 4.1 \\
\hline
352 \\
+\ \ 14080 \\
\hline
14432
\end{array}
$$

→ Note that there are 3 total decimal places in the two numbers.

→ We place the decimal 3 places in from the left.

Thus, the final product is 14.432.

Example: A shopper has 5 one-dollar bills, 6 quarters, 3 nickels, and 4 pennies in his pocket. How much money does he have?

$$5 \times \$1.00 = \$5.00$$

$$
\begin{array}{ccc}
3 & & \\
\$0.25 & \$0.05 & \$0.01 \\
\times\ \ 6 & \times\ \ 3 & \times\ \ 4 \\
\hline
\$1.50 & \$0.15 & \$0.04
\end{array}
$$

Note the placement of the decimals in the multiplication products. Thus, the total amount of money in the shopper's pocket is:

$$
\begin{array}{r}
\$5.00 \\
1.50 \\
0.15 \\
+\ \ 0.04 \\
\hline
\$6.69
\end{array}
$$

Division of Decimals

When dividing decimal numbers, we first remove the decimal in the divisor by moving the decimal in the dividend the same number of spaces to the right. For example, when dividing 1.45 into 5.3 we convert the numbers to 145 and 530 and perform normal whole number division.

Example: Find the quotient of 5.3 divided by 1.45.
             Convert to 145 and 530.

             Divide.

$$
\begin{array}{r}
3 \\
145\overline{)530} \\
-435 \\
\hline
95
\end{array}
\longrightarrow
\begin{array}{r}
3.65 \\
145\overline{)530.00} \\
-435 \\
\hline
950 \\
-870 \\
\hline
800
\end{array}
$$

⟶ Note that we insert the decimal to continue division.

Because one of the numbers divided contained one decimal place, we round the quotient to one decimal place. Thus, the final quotient is 3.7.

Applied Problem Solving

The most common use of decimals in everyday life is money. Consider the following problem dealing with a money transaction.

Question: A shopper has 5 one-dollar bills, 6 quarters, 3 nickels, and 4 pennies in his pocket. How much money does he have?

Solution:

$$
5 \times \$1.00 = \$5.00 \qquad
\begin{array}{r}
3 \\
\$0.25 \\
\times\ 6 \\
\hline
\$1.50
\end{array}
\quad
\begin{array}{r}
\$0.05 \\
\times\ 3 \\
\hline
\$0.15
\end{array}
\quad
\begin{array}{r}
\$0.01 \\
\times\ 4 \\
\hline
\$0.04
\end{array}
$$

Note the placement of the decimals in the multiplication products. Thus, the total amount of money in the shopper's pocket is:

$$
\begin{array}{r}
\$5.00 \\
1.50 \\
0.15 \\
+\ 0.04 \\
\hline
\$6.69
\end{array}
$$

Skill 12.3   **Solves problems involving percents (e.g., grades, discounts)**

Percent means per 100 (%).

Example: 10 percent $= \dfrac{10}{100} = \dfrac{1}{10} = 0.1$

Example: 10 percent of 150 means $\dfrac{10}{100} \times \dfrac{150}{1} = 15$

Example: Add 75% of 25 to 10% of 1000.

$$75\% \text{ of } 25 = \frac{75}{100} \times \frac{25}{1} = \frac{75}{4} \times \frac{1}{1} = \frac{75}{4} = 18\frac{3}{4} \text{ and}$$

$$10\% \text{ of } 1000 = \frac{10}{100} \times \frac{1000}{1} = \frac{10}{1} \times \frac{10}{1} = 100$$

Adding the two numbers gives:

$$18\frac{3}{4} + 100 = 118\frac{3}{4} \text{ or } 118.75$$

Example: 5 is what percent of 20?

This is the same as converting $\dfrac{5}{20}$ to % form.

$$\frac{5}{20} \times \frac{100}{1} = \frac{5}{1} \times \frac{5}{1} = 25\%$$

Example: There are 64 dogs in the kennel. 48 are collies. What percent are collies?

Restate the problem.   48 is what percent of 64?
Write an equation. $48 = n \times 64$
Solve. $\frac{48}{64} = n$

$n = \frac{3}{4} = 75\%$

75% of the dogs are collies.

Example: The auditorium was filled to 90% capacity. There were 558 seats occupied. What is the capacity of the auditorium?

Restate the problem.   90% of what number is 558?
Write an equation. $0.9n = 558$
Solve. $n = \frac{558}{.9}$
                        $n = 620$

The capacity of the auditorium is 620 people.

Example: A pair of shoes costs $42.00. Sales tax is 6%. What is the total cost of the shoes?

Restate the problem.   What is 6% of 42?
Write an equation. $n = 0.06 \times 42$
Solve. $n = 2.52$

Add the sales tax to the cost. $42.00 + $2.52 = $44.52

The total cost of the shoes, including sales tax, is $44.52.

Skill 12.4   Solves problems involving conversions between fractions, decimals, and percents

A **decimal** can be converted to a **percent** by multiplying by 100, or merely moving the decimal point two places to the right. A **percent** can be converted to a **decimal** by dividing by 100, or moving the decimal point two places to the left.

Examples: 0.375 = 37.5%
            0.7 = 70%
            0.04 = 4 %
            3.15 = 315 %
            84% = 0.84
            3 % = 0.03
            60% = 0.6
            110% = 1.1
            $\frac{1}{2}$% = 0.5% = 0.005

A **percent** can be converted to a **fraction** by placing it over 100 and reducing to simplest terms.

Example: Convert 0.056 to a fraction.

Multiplying 0.056 by $\dfrac{1000}{1000}$ to get rid of the decimal point:

$$0.056 \times \frac{1000}{1000} = \frac{56}{1000} = \frac{7}{125}$$

Example: Find 23% of 1000.

$$= \frac{23}{100} \times \frac{1000}{1} = 23 \times 10 = 230$$

Example: Convert 6.25% to a decimal and to a fraction.

$$6.25\% = 0.0625 = 0.0625 \times \frac{10000}{10000} = \frac{625}{10000} = \frac{1}{16}$$

Example: Find the decimal equivalent of $\dfrac{7}{10}$.

$$
\begin{array}{r}
.7 \\
10\overline{)7.0} \\
\underline{70} \\
00
\end{array}
$$

Since 10 cannot divide into 7 evenly, put a decimal point in the answer row on top; put a zero behind 7 to make it 70. Continue the division process. If a remainder occurs, put a zero by the last digit of the remainder and continue the division.

Thus $\dfrac{7}{10} = 0.7$

It is a good idea to write a zero before the decimal point so that the decimal point is emphasized.

Example: Find the decimal equivalent of $\frac{7}{125}$.

$$\begin{array}{r} .056 \\ 125\overline{)7.000} \\ 625 \\ 750 \\ 750 \\ 0 \end{array}$$

An example of a type of problem involving fractions is the conversion of recipes. For example, if a recipe serves 8 people and we want to make enough to serve only 4, we must determine how much of each ingredient to use. The conversion factor, the number we multiply each ingredient by, is:

$$\text{Conversion Factor} = \frac{\text{Number of Servings Needed}}{\text{Number of Servings in Recipe}}$$

Example: Consider the following recipe.

3 cups flour
½ tsp. baking powder
2/3 cups butter
2 cups sugar
2 eggs

If the above recipe serves 8, how much of each ingredient do we need to serve only 4 people?

First, determine the conversion factor.

Conversion Factor = $\frac{4}{8} = \frac{1}{2}$

Next, multiply each ingredient by the conversion factor.

3 x ½ =	1 ½ cups flour
½ x ½ =	¼ tsp. baking powder
2/3 x ½ = 2/6 =	1/3 cups butter
2 x ½ =	1 cup sugar
2 x ½ =	1 egg

Sample Test

DIRECTIONS: Read the following paragraph and answer the questions that follow.

This writer has often been asked to tutor hospitalized children with cystic fibrosis. While undergoing all the precautionary measures to see these children (i.e. scrubbing thoroughly and donning sterilized protective gear- for the child's protection), she has often wondered why their parents subject these children to the pressures of schooling and trying to catch up on what they have missed because of hospitalization, which is a normal part of cystic fibrosis patients' lives. These children undergo so many tortuous treatments a day that it seems cruel to expect them to learn as normal children do, especially with their life expectancies being as short as they are.

1. **What is meant by the word "precautionary" in the second sentence?**
   (Average Rigor) (Skill 1.1)

   A. Careful
   B. Protective
   C. Medical
   D. Sterilizing

2. **Which word is a not synonym for "donning"?**
   (Easy) (Skill 1.2)

   A. To wear
   B. To put on
   C. To prepare
   D. To don

3. **What is the main idea of this passage?**
   (Average Rigor) (Skill 2.1)

   A. There is a lot of preparation involved in visiting a patient of cystic fibrosis.
   B. Children with cystic fibrosis are incapable of living normal lives.
   C. Certain concessions should be made for children with cystic fibrosis.
   D. Children with cystic fibrosis die young.

4. **Which of the following sentences is the best summary statement for this passage?**
   (Rigorous) (Skill 2.2)

   A. This writer has often been asked to tutor hospitalized children with cystic fibrosis.
   B. These children undergo so many tortuous treatments a day that it seems cruel to expect them to learn as normal children do, especially with their life expectancies being as short as they are.
   C. While undergoing all the precautionary measures to see these children (i.e. scrubbing thoroughly and donning sterilized protective gear- for the child's protection), she has often wondered why their parents subject these children to the pressures of schooling and trying to catch up on what they have missed because of hospitalization, which is a normal part of cystic fibrosis patients' lives.

5. **The author states that it is "cruel" to expect children with cystic fibrosis to learn as "normal" children do. Is this a fact or an opinion?**
   (Average Rigor) (Skill 4.3)

   A.   Fact
   B.   Opinion

DIRECTIONS: Read the following passage and answer the questions that follow.

Disciplinary practices have been found to affect diverse areas of child development such as the acquisition of moral values, obedience to authority, and performance at school. Even though the dictionary has a specific Definition of the word "discipline," it is still open to interpretation by people of different cultures.

There are four types of disciplinary styles: assertion of power, withdrawal of love, reasoning, and permissiveness. Assertion of power involves the use of force to discourage unwanted behavior. Withdrawal of love involves making the love of a parent conditional on a child's good behavior. Reasoning involves persuading the child to behave one way rather than another. Permissiveness involves allowing the child to do as he or she pleases and face the consequences of his/her actions.

6. **What is the meaning of the word "diverse" in the first sentence?**
   (Easy) (Skill 1.1)

   A.   Many
   B.   Related to children
   C.   Disciplinary
   D.   Moral

7. **Which of the following words is an antonym of "assertion"?**
    (Average Rigor) (Skill 1.2)

    A. denial
    B. allegation
    C. contention
    D. affirmation

8. **Which of the following words is a synonym of "permissiveness"?**
    (Rigorous) (Skill 1.2)

    A. narrow-mindedness
    B. intolerance
    C. tolerance
    D. insularity

9. **What is the main idea of this passage?**
    (Average Rigor) (Skill 2.1)

    A. Different people have different ideas of what discipline is.
    B. Permissiveness is the most widely used disciplinary style.
    C. Most people agree on their definition of discipline.
    D. There are four disciplinary styles.

10. **Consider the following sentence:**

    There are four types of disciplinary styles.

    What type of sentence is it?
    (Rigorous) (Skill 2.3)

    A. Summary statement
    B. Explanatory statement
    C. Supporting statement
    D. Introductory statement

11. **Name the four types of disciplinary styles.**
    (Easy) (Skill 3.1)

    A. Reasoning, power assertion, morality, and permissiveness.
    B. Morality, reasoning, permissiveness, and withdrawal of love.
    C. Withdrawal of love, permissiveness, assertion of power, and reasoning.
    D. Permissiveness, morality, reasoning, and power assertion.

12. Consider the following statement from the passage:

"Disciplinary practices have been found to affect diverse areas of child development such as the acquisition of moral values, obedience to authority, and performance at school."

Which statement best reflects the author's attitude toward a possible cause-effect relationship between child development and discipline?
(Rigorous) (Skill 3.3)

A. There is no relationship between discipline and child development.
B. Disciplinary practices explain child behavior.
C. Child development is impacted by disciplinary practices.

13. The author states that "assertion of power involves the use of force to discourage unwanted behavior." Is this a fact or an opinion?
(Average Rigor) (Skill 4.3)

A. Fact
B. Opinion

DIRECTIONS: Read the following passage and answer the questions that follow.

One of the most difficult problems plaguing American education is the assessment of teachers. No one denies that teachers ought to be answerable for what they do, but what exactly does that mean? The Oxford American Dictionary defines accountability as: the obligation to give a reckoning or explanation for one's actions.

Does a student have to learn for teaching to have taken place? Historically, teaching has not been defined in this restrictive manner; the teacher was thought to be responsible for the quantity and quality of material covered and the way in which it was presented. However, some definitions of teaching now imply that students must learn in order for teaching to have taken place.

As a teacher who tries my best to keep current on all the latest teaching strategies, I believe that those teachers who do not bother even to pick up an educational journal every once in a while should be kept under close watch. There are many teachers out there who have been teaching for decades and refuse to change their ways even if research has proven that their methods are outdated and ineffective. There is no place in the profession of teaching for these types of individuals. It is time that the American educational system clean house, for the sake of our children.

14. What is meant by the word "plaguing" in the first sentence?
(Easy) (Skill 1.1)

   A.   Causing problems
   B.   Causing illness
   C.   Causing anger
   D.   Causing failure

15. What is the meaning of the word "reckoning" in the third sentence?
(Average Rigor) (Skill 1.1)

   A.   Thought
   B.   Answer
   C.   Obligation
   D.   Explanation

16. Which word is an antonym of "bountiful"?
(Average Rigor) (Skill 1.2)

   A.   profuse
   B.   abundant
   C.   copious
   D.   scarce

17. What is the main idea of the passage?
(Average Rigor) (Skill 2.1)

   A.   Teachers should not be answerable for what they do.
   B.   Teachers who do not do their job should be fired.
   C.   The author is a good teacher.
   D.   Assessment of teachers is a serious problem in society today.

18. Which of the following statements is the topic sentence for paragraph three?
(Easy) (Skill 2.2)

A. As a teacher who tries my best to keep current on all the latest teaching strategies, I believe that those teachers who do not bother even to pick up an educational journal every once in a while should be kept under close watch.

B. There are many teachers out there who have been teaching for decades and refuse to change their ways even if research has proven that their methods are outdated and ineffective.

C. There is no place in the profession of teaching for these types of individuals.

D. It is time that the American educational system clean house, for the sake of our children.

19. **Which of the following sentences is the best summary statement for this passage?**
(Rigorous) (Skill 2.2)

A. One of the most difficult problems plaguing American education is the assessment of teachers.
B. However, some definitions of teaching now imply that students must learn in order for teaching to have taken place.
C. It is time that the American educational system clean house, for the sake of our children.

20. **The author states that teacher assessment is a problem for**
(Easy) (Skill 2.3)

A. Elementary schools
B. Secondary schools
C. American education
D. Families

21. **Teachers who do not keep current on educational trends should be fired. Is this a fact or an opinion?**
(Average Rigor) (Skill 4.3)

A. Fact
B. Opinion

Mr. Smith gave instructions for the painting to be hung on the wall. And then it leaped forth before his eyes: the little cottages on the river, the white clouds floating over the valley and the green of the towering mountain ranges which were seen in the distance. The painting was so vivid that it seemed almost real. Mr. Smith was now absolutely certain that the painting had been the worth the money.

22. **What is the meaning of the word "vivid" in the third sentence?**
(Average Rigor) (Skill 1.1)

A. Lifelike
B. Dark
C. Expensive
D. Big

23. **What does the author mean by the expression "it leaped forth before his eyes"?**
(Rigorous) (Skill 1.1)

A. The painting fell off the wall.
B. The painting appeared so real it was almost three-dimensional.
C. The painting struck Mr. Smith in the face.
D. Mr. Smith was hallucinating.

24. **What is the main idea of this passage?**
(Average Rigor) (Skill 2.1)

   A. The painting that Mr. Smith purchased is expensive.
   B. Mr. Smith purchased a painting.
   C. Mr. Smith was pleased with the quality of the painting he had purchased.
   D. The painting depicted cottages and valleys.

25. **Select the correct word to complete the sentence correctly.**
(Rigorous) (Skill 1.3)

   He _____ her backpack down near the bin filled with shoes.

   A. sat
   B. set
   C. sets

26. **Select the correct combination of words to complete the sentence correctly.**
(Rigorous) (Skill 1.3)

   _____ you and me, our grandfather cannot tell the difference _____ those triplets.

   A. Between, between
   B. Between, amongst
   C. Between, among

27. **Select the correct word to complete the sentence correctly.**
(Rigorous) (Skill 1.3)

   The move from Idaho to Chicago _____ the young boy in many ways.

   A. affected
   B. effects
   C. effected

28. **Organize the following set of instructions into its proper sequence.**
(Average Rigor) (Skill 3.2)

   1. Pick up the knife, dip it into the peanut butter, and spread it on one slice of bread.

   2. Press the two pieces together and serve.

   3. On the other slice of bread, spread your favorite jelly.

   4. Put the spoon down.

   5. Remove two pieces of bread from the bag and set them on the counter.

   6. Put the knife down.

   7. Open the jelly and pick up the spoon.

   A. 7, 3, 2, 1, 6, 2, 4
   B. 5, 7, 3, 1, 6, 4, 2
   C. 5, 1, 6, 7, 3, 4, 2

29. Organize the following set of instructions into its proper sequence.
(Rigorous) (Skill 3.2)

1. Remove the spare tire from its location, obtain the jack, and lug wrench.

2. Pry off the flat tire's hubcap using the sharp end of the lug wrench, a screwdriver, or a utility knife.

3. Place the car in "park" and apply the parking brake.

4. To loosen each lug nut, turn the wrench counterclockwise about one turn while the tire is still on the ground.

5. Finally, use the wrench to tighten each lug nut tightly.

6. Jack up the car until the flat tire is several inches off the ground, providing enough clearance to remove the tire.

7. Remove the lug nuts and remove the wheel.

8. Pull safely off the road.

9. Replace the lug nuts and tighten each lightly.

10. Lower the car to the ground and remove the jack.

11. Lift the spare tire onto the axle hub and align the holes.

12. Place the jack under the reinforced section of the car's body.

A. 3, 1, 2, 4, 6, 7, 11, 12, 8, 9, 10, 5

B. 8, 3, 1, 2, 4, 12, 6, 7, 11, 9, 10, 5

C. 8, 1, 3, 12, 6, 2, 7, 4, 11, 10, 9, 5

30. Consider the data in the bar graph below. Which of the following statements is true? *(Average Rigor) (Skill 4.1)*

Graduation Rates 2003

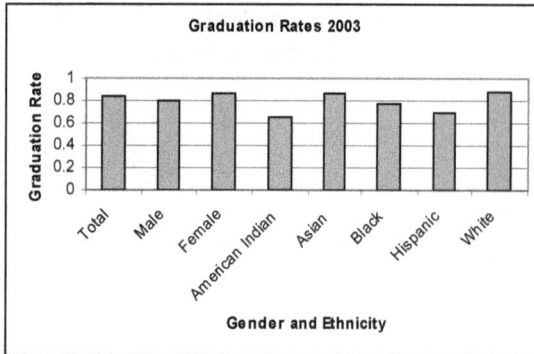

A. More males graduated in 2003 than females.

B. In 2003, American Indian and Black students held the lowest graduation rate.

C. Based on this information, one could infer that Hispanics had the highest dropout rate.

D. Female, Asian, and white students had the highest graduation rates.

31. Consider the data in the bar graph below. Which of the following statements is *not* true? *(Rigorous) (Skill 4.1)*

Statewide Trends in Assaults and Fights

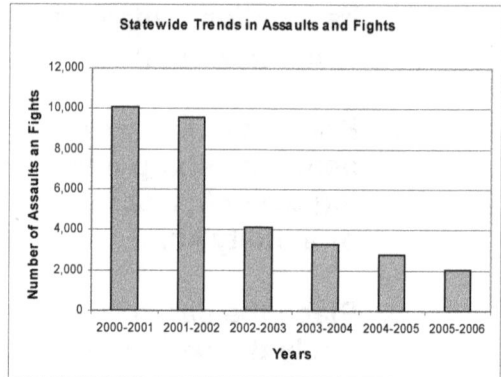

A. One could infer that anti-bullying programs in K-12 schools helped decrease physical violence.

B. Over the six-year period, the number of assaults or fights decreased by about 40%.

C. Over the six-year period, the number of assaults or fights decreased by about 80%.

D. The 2002-2003 school year showed a sharp decline in physical violence.

32. **Consider the data in the pie chart below. Which of the following is *not* true? (Rigorous) (Skill 4.1)**

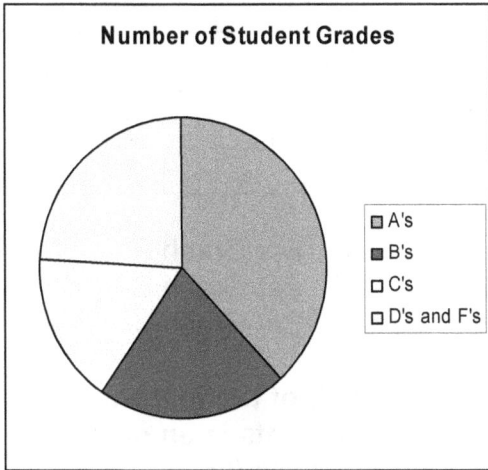

Number of Student Grades

- A's
- B's
- C's
- D's and F's

    A. Nearly 1/3 of these students received a B or a C.

    B. Nearly 30% of this teacher's students failed this grading period.

    C. This teacher may need to challenge high-achieving students more.

    D. This teacher may need to find ways to motivate underachieving students.

33. The following is a set of data from a class of students who completed a survey on learning styles and strengths. Which bar graph shows the correct data for this class?
(Average Rigor) (Skill 4.2)

Section	Total
I	2
II	4
III	8
IV	7
V	3
VI	6
VII	0
VIII	1

Bar Graph A

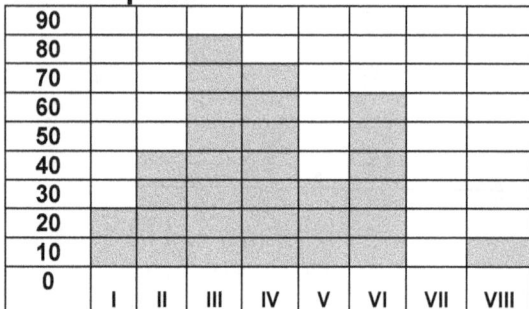

Bar Graph B

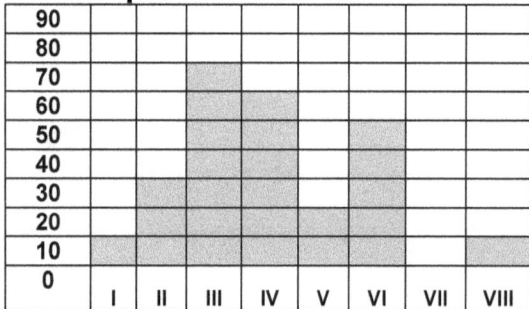

Bar Graph C

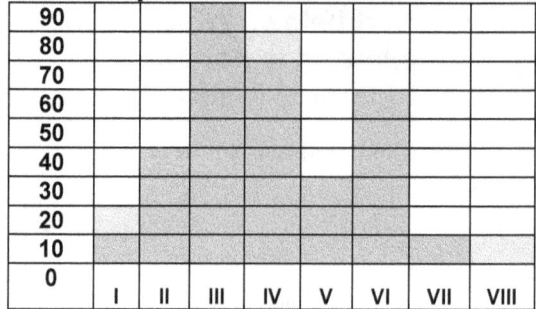

A. Bar Graph A
B. Bar Graph B
C. Bar Graph C

34. Which of the following statements is an opinion?
(Easy) (Skill 4.3)

A. Frogs are amphibians.
B. When fall weather turns cold, it's best to dress in layers.
C. Blue and yellow make green.
D. Her living room décor seems ancient.

DIRECTIONS : *The passage below contains many errors. Read the passage. Then answer each test item by choosing the option that corrects an error in the underlined portion(s). No more than one underlined error will appear in each item. If no error exists, choose "No change is necessary."*

Climbing to the top of Mount Everest is an adventure. One which everyone--whether physically fit or not--seems eager to try. The trail stretches for miles, the cold temperatures are usually frigid and brutal.

Climbers must endure severel barriers on the way, including other hikers, steep jagged rocks, and lots of snow. Plus, climbers often find the most grueling part of the trip is their climb back down, just when they are feeling greatly exhausted. Climbers who take precautions are likely to find the ascent less arduous than the unprepared. By donning heavy flannel shirts, gloves, and hats, climbers prevented hypothermia, as well as simple frostbite. A pair of rugged boots is also one of the necesities. If climbers are to avoid becoming dehydrated, there is beverages available for them to transport as well.

Once climbers are completely ready to begin there lengthy journey, they can comfortably enjoy the wonderful scenery. Wide rock formations dazzle the observers eyes with shades of gray and white, while the peak forms a triangle that seems to touch the sky. Each of the climbers are reminded of the splendor and magnifisence of Gods great Earth.

35. **Each of the climbers <u>are</u> reminded of the splendor and <u>magnifisence</u> of <u>God's</u> great Earth.**
   (Rigorous) (Skill 5.1)

   A. is
   B. magnifisence
   C. Gods
   D. No change is necessary

36. **Plus, climbers often find the most grueling part of the trip is <u>their</u> climb back <u>down, just</u> when they <u>are</u> feeling greatly exhausted.**
   (Average Rigor) (Skill 5.2)

   A. his
   B. down; just
   C. were
   D. No change is necessary

37. **Once climbers are completely prepared for <u>there</u> lengthy <u>journey, they</u> can comfortably enjoy the <u>wonderful</u> scenery.**
   (Average Rigor) (Skill 6.2)

   A. wonderfull
   B. journey; they
   C. their
   D. No change is necessary

38. **<u>Climbers who</u> take precautions are likely to find the ascent <u>less difficult</u> <u>than</u> the unprepared.**
   (Average Rigor) (Skill 6.3)

   A. Climbers, who
   B. least difficult
   C. then
   D. No change is necessary

39. Climbing to the top of Mount Everest is an <u>adventure. One</u> which everyone —<u>whether</u> physically fit or not—<u>seems</u> eager to try.
(Rigorous) (Skill 7.3)

   A. adventure, one
   B. people, whether
   C. seem
   D. No change is necessary

40. The <u>trail</u> stretches for <u>miles,</u> the cold temperatures are <u>usually</u> frigid and brutal.
(Rigorous) (Skill 7.3)

   A. trails
   B. miles;
   C. usual
   D. No change is necessary

41. Climbers must endure <u>severel</u> barriers <u>on the way,</u> <u>including</u> other <u>hikers,</u> steep jagged rocks, and lots of snow.
(Easy) (Skill 8.3)

   A. several
   B. on the way: including
   C. hikers'
   D. No change is necessary

42. A pair of rugged boots <u>is</u> <u>also one</u> of the <u>necesities</u>.
(Rigorous) (Skill 8.3)

   A. are
   B. also, one
   C. necessities
   D. No change is necessary

DIRECTIONS: *The passage below contains several errors. Read the passage. Then answer each test item by choosing the option that corrects an error in the underlined portion(s). No more than one underlined error will appear in each item. If no error exists, choose "No change is necessary."*

Every job places different kinds of demands on their employees. For example, whereas such jobs as accounting and bookkeeping require mathematical ability; graphic design requires creative/artistic ability.

Doing good at one job does not usually guarantee success at another. However, one of the elements crucial to all jobs are especially notable: the chance to accomplish a goal.

The accomplishment of the employees varies according to the job. In many jobs the employees become accustom to the accomplishment provided by the work they do every day.

In medicine, for example, every doctor tests him self by treating badly injured or critically ill people. In the operating room, a team of Surgeons is responsible for operating on many of these patients. In addition to the feeling of accomplishment that the workers achieve, some jobs also give a sense of identity to the employees'. Profesions like law, education, and sales offer huge financial and emotional rewards. Politicians are public servants: who work for the federal and state governments. President bush is basically employed by the American people to make laws and run the country.

Finally; the contributions that employees make to their companies and to the world cannot be taken for granted. Through their work, employees are performing a service for their employers and are contributing something to the world.

43. **However, one of the elements crucial to all jobs are especially notable: the accomplishment of a goal.**
(Rigorous) (Skill 5.1)

   A. However
   B. is
   C. notable;
   D. No change is necessary

44. **The accomplishment of the employees varies according to the job.**
(Rigorous) (Skill 5.1)

   A. accomplishment,
   B. employee's
   C. vary
   D. No change is necessary

45. **In many jobs the employees become accustom to the accomplishment provided by the work they do every day.**
(Average Rigor) (Skill 5.2)

   A. became
   B. accustomed
   C. provides
   D. No change is necessary

46. **In medicine, for example, every doctor tests him self by treating badly injured and critically ill people.**
(Average Rigor) (Skill 6.1)

   A. test
   B. himself
   C. critical
   D. No change is necessary

47. **Every job places different kinds of demands on their employees.**
(Rigorous) (Skill 6.2)

   A. place
   B. its
   C. employes
   D. No change is necessary

48. **Doing good at one job does not usually guarantee success at another.**
(Rigorous) (Skill 6.3)

   A. well
   B. usualy
   C. succeeding
   D. No change is necessary

49. **Politicians are public servants: who work for the federal and state governments.**
(Easy) (Skill 7.3)

   A. were
   B. servants who
   C. worked
   D. No change is necessary

50. For example, whereas such jobs as accounting and bookkeeping require mathematical ability; graphic design requires creative/artistic ability.
(Average Rigor) (Skill 7.3)

A. For example
B. whereas,
C. ability,
D. No change is necessary

51. In addition to the feeling of accomplishment that the workers achieve, some jobs also give a sense of self-identity to the employees'.
(Average Rigor) (Skill 7.3)

A. acheive
B. gave
C. employees
D. No change is necessary

52. Finally; the contributions that employees make to their companies and to the world cannot be taken for granted.
(Average Rigor) (Skill 7.3)

A. Finally,
B. their
C. took
D. No change is necessary

53. In the operating room, a team of Surgeons is responsible for operating on many of these patients.
(Easy) (Skill 8.2)

A. operating room:
B. surgeons is
C. those
D. No change is necessary

54. President bush is basically employed by the American people to make laws and run the country.
(Easy) (Skill 8.2)

A. Bush
B. to
C. made
D. No change is necessary

55. Profesions like law, education, and sales offer huge financial and emotional rewards.
(Average Rigor) (Skill 8.3)

A. Professions
B. education;
C. offered
D. No change is necessary

56. **Choose the sentence that demonstrates correct verb tense.**
(Average Rigor) (Skill 5.2)

    A. He should have went to the store last night.
    B. He should of went to the store last night.
    C. He should of gone to the store last night.
    D. He should have gone to the store last night.

57. **Choose the sentence that logically and correctly expresses the comparison.**
(Easy) (Skill 6.3)

    A. The Empire State Building in New York is taller than buildings in the city.

    B. The Empire State Building in New York is taller than any other building in the city.

    C. The Empire State Building in New York is tallest than other buildings in the city.

58. **Identify the complete sentence below.**
(Average Rigor) (Skill 7.1)

    A. The pastor waiting for the offering basket to be passed through the crowd.

    B. Growling at the back door as her owner hoped the cat would leave.

    C. He didn't finish mowing the lawn, so he couldn't attend the birthday party.

    D. By paying too much attention to interest surveys can make a teacher unaware of students' academic needs.

59. **Choose the sentence that is complete and written correctly. (Rigorous) (Skill 7.1)**

   A. Even though there are a number of different methods for helping the patient overcome a dependency.

   B. Even though different methods can help a patient overcome a dependency, there is no way to know which is best in the long-run.

   C. Even though there is no way to know which way is best patients can overcome their dependencies when they are helped.

   D. None of these sentences is correct.

60. **Choose the sentence that is complete and written correctly. (Rigorous) (Skill 7.2)**

   A. There are too many or too few qualified candidates for a certain position, and then they have to be confirmed by the Senate where there is the possibility of rejection.

   B. Either there are too many or too few qualified candidate for a certain position then they have to be confirmed by the Senate, where there is the possibility of rejection.

   C. The Senate has to confirm qualified candidates, who face the possibility of rejection.

   D. Because the Senate has to confirm qualified candidates; they face the possibility of rejection.

61. A run-on sentence is listed below. Choose the item that shows the correct sentence structure.
(Rigorous) (Skill 7.2)

I made the cookies I didn't clean up the kitchen.

A. I made the cookies, but I didn't clean up the kitchen.

B. After I made the cookies I didn't clean up the kitchen.

C. I didn't clean up the kitchen, I made the cookies.

62. Choose the sentence that is complete and written correctly.
(Rigorous) (Skill 7.3)

A. Overcrowding budget cutbacks and societal deterioration have greatly affected student learning.

B. Student learning has been greatly affected by overcrowding, budget cutbacks, and societal deterioration.

C. Due to overcrowding, budget cutbacks, and societal deterioration student learning has been greatly affected.

D. None of these sentences is correct.

63. Select the underline section that is capitalized correctly.

the bombing of the Oklahoma City Federal Building was considered to be one of the worst Terrorist incidents on American Soil
(Easy) (Skill 8.2)

A. the bombing

B. Oklahoma City Federal Building

C. Terrorist

D. American Soil

64. Select the underline section that is capitalized correctly.

The Flu epidemic struck most of the respected faculty and students of the Woolbright School, forcing the Boynton Beach School Superintendent to close it down for two weeks.
(Average Rigor) (Skill 8.2)

A. Flu

B. the Woolbright School

C. Boynton Beach School Superintendent

D. None of these is capitalized correctly.

65. Round $1\frac{13}{16}$ of an inch to the nearest quarter of an inch.
(Average Rigor) (Skill 9.2)

A. $1\frac{1}{4}$ inch

B. $1\frac{5}{8}$ inch

C. $1\frac{3}{4}$ inch

D. 2 inches

66. What unit of measurement could we use to report the distance traveled walking around a track?
(Easy) (Skill 9.3)

A. degrees

B. square meters

C. kilometers

D. cubic feet

67. What unit of measurement would describe the spread of a forest fire in a unit time?
(Average Rigor) (Skill 9.3)

A. 10 square yards per second

B. 10 yards per minute

C. 10 feet per hour

D. 10 cubit feet per hour

68. 3 km is equivalent to
(Average Rigor) (Skill 9.3)

A. 300 cm

B. 300 m

C. 3000 cm

D. 3000 m

69. The mass of a cookie is closest to:
(Rigorous) (Skill 9.3)

A. 0.5 kg

B. 0.5 grams

C. 15 grams

D. 1.5 grams

70. The following chart shows the yearly average number of international tourists visiting Palm Beach for 1990-1994. How many more international tourists visited Palm Beach in 1994 than in 1991?
(Average Rigor) (Skill 10.2)

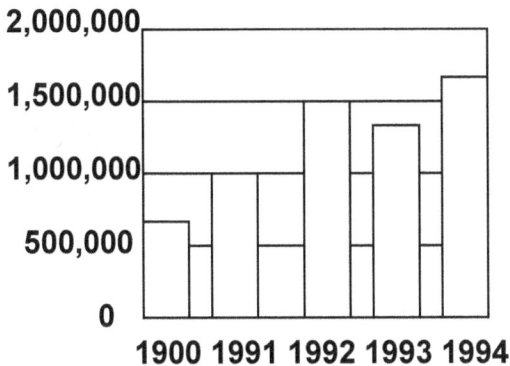

A. 100,000

B. 600,000

C. 1,600,000

D. 8,000,000

71. (576 + 29) − (52 − 27) =
(Easy) (Skill 10.3)

A. 580

B. 526

C. 680

D. 589

72. 1250 ÷ 50 =
(Easy) (Skill 11.2)

A. 20

B. 25

C. 15

D. 40

73. A sofa sells for $520. If the retailer makes a 30% profit, what was the wholesale price?
(Rigorous) (Skill 11.3)

A. $400
B. $676
C. $490
D. $364

74. The price of gas was $3.27 per gallon. Your tank holds 15 gallons of fuel. You are using two tanks a week. How much will you save weekly if the price of gas goes down to $2.30 per gallon?
(Average Rigor) (Skill 11.3)

A. $26.00

B. $29.00

C. $15.00

D. $17.00

75. Two mathematics classes have a total of 410 students. The 8:00 am class has 40 more than the 10:00 am class. How many students are in the 10:00 am class?
(Rigorous) (Skill 11.3)

    A.   123.3

    B.   370

    C.   185

    D.   330

76. If $4x - (3 - x) = 7(x - 3) + 10$, then
(Rigorous) (Skill 11.3)

    A. $x = 8$

    B. $x = -8$

    C. $x = 4$

    D. $x = -4$

77. $\dfrac{7}{9} + \dfrac{1}{3} \div \dfrac{2}{3} =$
(Average Rigor) (Skill 12.1)

    A. $\dfrac{5}{3}$

    B. $\dfrac{3}{2}$

    C.   2

    D. $\dfrac{23}{18}$

78. Which statement is true about George's budget?
(Average Rigor) (Skill 12.1)

    A.   George spends the greatest portion of his income on food.

    B.   George spends twice as much on utilities as he does on his mortgage.

    C.   George spends twice as much on utilities as he does on food.

    D.   George spends the same amount on food and utilities as he does on his mortgage.

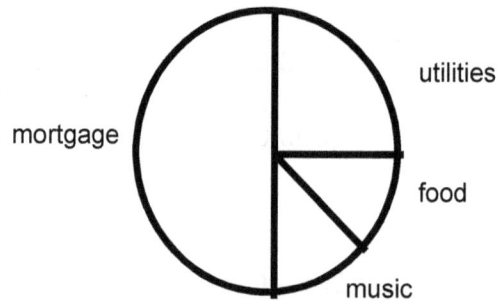

79. $\left(\dfrac{^-4}{9}\right) + \left(\dfrac{^-7}{10}\right) =$
(Rigorous) (Skill 12.1)

    A. $\dfrac{23}{90}$

    B. $\dfrac{^-23}{90}$

    C. $\dfrac{103}{90}$

    D. $\dfrac{^-103}{90}$

80. $4\dfrac{2}{9} \times \dfrac{7}{10}$

    (Rigorous) (Skill 12.1)

    A. $4\dfrac{9}{10}$

    B. $\dfrac{266}{90}$

    C. $2\dfrac{43}{45}$

    D. $2\dfrac{6}{20}$

81. $(5.6) \times (^-0.11) =$

    (Average Rigor) (Skill 12.2)

    A. $^-0.616$

    B. 0.616

    C. $^-6.110$

    D. 6.110

82. An item that sells for $375 is put on sale at $120. What is the percent of decrease?
    (Rigorous) (Skill 12.3)

    A. 25%

    B. 28%

    C. 68%

    D. 34%

83. A movie theater has a 500-person capacity. At the start of a movie, 457 seats were taken. By the end of the movie, 96 people had left early. What was the percent change in occupied seats from the beginning to the end of the movie?
    (Rigorous) (Skill 12.3)

    A. 15%

    B. 17%

    C. 19.2%

    D. 19.7%

84. $0.74 =$
    (Easy) (Skill 12.4)

    A. $\dfrac{74}{100}$

    B. 7.4%

    C. $\dfrac{33}{50}$

    D. $\dfrac{74}{10}$

85. 303 is what percent of 600?
    (Easy) (Skill 12.4)

    A. 0.505%

    B. 5.05%

    C. 505%

    D. 50.5%

86. Jim must deliver 65% of his campaign flyers by the end of the week. If he has 700 flyers, how many must he deliver to meet this requirement?
(Average Rigor) (Skill 12.4)

   A.   475 flyers

   B.   425 flyers

   C.   435 flyers

   D.   455 flyers

87. A restaurant employs 465 people. There are 280 waiters and 185 cooks. If 168 waiters and 85 cooks receive pay raises, what percent of the waiters will receive a pay raise?
(Average Rigor) (Skill 12.4)

   A.   36.13%

   B.   60%

   C.   60.22%

   D.   40%

88. Choose the equation that is equivalent to the following:

$$\frac{3x}{5} - 5 = 5x$$

(Rigorous) (Skill 12.4)

   A. $3x - 25 = 25x$

   B. $x - \dfrac{25}{3} = 25x$

   C. $6x - 50 = 75x$

   D. $x + 25 = 25x$

89. In a sample of 40 full-time employees at a particular company, 35 were also holding down a part-time job requiring at least 10 hours/week. If this proportion holds for the entire company of 25000 employees, how many full-time employees at this company are actually holding down a part-time job of at least 10 hours per week.
(Rigorous) (Skill 12.4)

   A.   714

   B.   625

   C.   21,875

   D.   28,571

90. **Consider the following recipe ingredients for a dish that serves eight people:**

    one 3 ½-pound chicken
    ½ teaspoon of thyme
    7 tablespoons butter

    What would the correct amounts be to only serve 4 people?
    (Rigorous) (Skill 12.4)

    A.   1.6 pounds of chicken,
         ¼ teaspoon of thyme,
         3 ¾ tablespoons of
         butter

    B.   1.8 pounds of chicken,
         ¼ teaspoon of thyme,
         3 ½ tablespoons of
         butter

    C.   1 ¾ pounds of chicken,
         ¼ teaspoon of thyme,
         3 ½ tablespoons of
         butter

    D.   1 ¾ pounds of chicken,
         ¼ teaspoon of thyme,
         3 ¼ tablespoons of
         butter

Answer Key

1.	B	31.	B	61.	A
2.	C	32.	B	62.	B
3.	C	33.	A	63.	B
4.	C	34.	D	64.	C
5.	B	35.	A	65.	C
6.	A	36.	D	66.	C
7.	A	37.	C	67.	A
8.	C	38.	D	68.	D
9.	A	39.	A	69.	C
10.	D	40.	B	70.	B
11.	C	41.	A	71.	A
12.	C	42.	C	72.	B
13.	A	43.	B	73.	A
14.	A	44.	C	74.	B
15.	D	45.	B	75.	C
16.	D	46.	B	76.	C
17.	D	47.	B	77.	D
18.	A	48.	A	78.	C
19.	C	49.	B	79.	D
20.	C	50.	C	80.	C
21.	B	51.	C	81.	A
22.	A	52.	A	82.	C
23.	B	53.	B	83.	C
24.	C	54.	A	84.	A
25.	B	55.	A	85.	D
26.	C	56.	D	86.	D
27.	C	57.	B	87.	B
28.	C	58.	C	88.	A
29.	B	59.	B	89.	C
30.	D	60.	C	90.	C

Rigor Table

	Easy 20%	Average 40%	Rigorous 40%
Questions (90)	2, 6, 11, 14, 18, 20, 34, 41, 49, 53, 54, 57, 63, 66, 72, 84, 85, 71	1, 3, 5, 9, 13, 15, 16, 17, 21, 22, 24, 28, 30, 33, 36, 37, 38, 45, 46, 50, 51, 52, 55, 56, 58, 64, 65, 67, 68, 70, 74, 77, 78, 81, 86, 87	4, 7, 8, 10, 12, 19, 23, 25, 26, 27, 29, 31, 32, 35, 39, 40, 42, 43, 44, 47, 48, 59, 60, 61, 62, 69, 73, 75, 76, 79, 80, 82, 83, 88, 89, 90
TOTALS	18 (20.0%)	36 (40.0%)	36 (40.0%)

Rationales with Sample Questions

DIRECTIONS: Read the following paragraph and answer the questions that follow.

This writer has often been asked to tutor hospitalized children with cystic fibrosis. While undergoing all the precautionary measures to see these children (i.e. scrubbing thoroughly and donning sterilized protective gear- for the child's protection), she has often wondered why their parents subject these children to the pressures of schooling and trying to catch up on what they have missed because of hospitalization, which is a normal part of cystic fibrosis patients' lives. These children undergo so many tortuous treatments a day that it seems cruel to expect them to learn as normal children do, especially with their life expectancies being as short as they are.

1. **What is meant by the word "precautionary" in the second sentence? (Average Rigor) (Skill 1.1)**

    A.   Careful
    B.   Protective
    C.   Medical
    D.   Sterilizing

Answer: B. Protective

The writer uses expressions such as "protective gear" and "child's protection" to emphasize this.

2. **Which word is a not synonym for "donning"? (Easy) (Skill 1.2)**

    A.   To wear
    B.   To put on
    C.   To prepare
    D.   To don

Answer: C. To prepare

A synonym is a different word with a similar meaning. To "don" something refers to putting it on or wearing it, not to prepare.

3.   **What is the main idea of this passage?**
     (Average Rigor) (Skill 2.1)

   A.   There is a lot of preparation involved in visiting a patient of cystic fibrosis.
   B.   Children with cystic fibrosis are incapable of living normal lives.
   C.   Certain concessions should be made for children with cystic fibrosis.
   D.   Children with cystic fibrosis die young.

Answer: C. Certain concessions should be made for children with cystic fibrosis.

The correct answer is C. The author states that she wonders "why parents subject these children to the pressures of schooling" and that "it seems cruel to expect them to learn as normal children do." In making these statements she appears to be expressing the belief that these children should not have to do what "normal" children do. They have enough to deal with – their illness itself.

4.   **Which of the following sentences is the best summary statement for this passage?**
     (Rigorous) (Skill 2.2)

   A. This writer has often been asked to tutor hospitalized children with cystic fibrosis.
   B. These children undergo so many tortuous treatments a day that it seems cruel to expect them to learn as normal children do, especially with their life expectancies being as short as they are.
   C. While undergoing all the precautionary measures to see these children (i.e. scrubbing thoroughly and donning sterilized protective gear- for the child's protection), she has often wondered why their parents subject these children to the pressures of schooling and trying to catch up on what they have missed because of hospitalization, which is a normal part of cystic fibrosis patients' lives.

Answer: C. While undergoing all the precautionary measures to see these children (i.e. scrubbing thoroughly and donning sterilized protective gear-for the child's protection), she has often wondered why their parents subject these children to the pressures of schooling and trying to catch up on what they have missed because of hospitalization, which is a normal part of cystic fibrosis patients' lives.

The summary statement is found at or near the end of the passage, and best sums up the author's main point.

5.   **The author states that it is "cruel" to expect children with cystic fibrosis to learn as "normal" children do. Is this a fact or an opinion?**
     (Average Rigor) (Skill 4.3)

   A.   Fact
   B.   Opinion

Answer: B. Opinion

The fact that the author states that it "seems" cruel indicates there is no evidence to support this belief.

DIRECTIONS: Read the following passage and answer the questions that follow.

Disciplinary practices have been found to affect diverse areas of child development such as the acquisition of moral values, obedience to authority, and performance at school. Even though the dictionary has a specific definition of the word "discipline," it is still open to interpretation by people of different cultures.

There are four types of disciplinary styles: assertion of power, withdrawal of love, reasoning, and permissiveness. Assertion of power involves the use of force to discourage unwanted behavior. Withdrawal of love involves making the love of a parent conditional on a child's good behavior. Reasoning involves persuading the child to behave one way rather than another. Permissiveness involves allowing the child to do as he or she pleases and face the consequences of his/her actions.

6. **What is the meaning of the word "diverse" in the first sentence? (Easy) (Skill 1.1)**

   A. Many
   B. Related to children
   C. Disciplinary
   D. Moral

Answer: A. Many

Being diverse refers to having variety or varying/different characteristics. None of the other choices are reasonable.

7. **Which of the following words is an antonym of "assertion"? (Average Rigor) (Skill 1.2)**

   A. denial
   B. allegation
   C. contention
   D. affirmation

Answer: A. denial

An antonym is a word that means the opposite of the first word. An assertion involves making a claim or allegation, holding something in contention, or giving an affirmation of something as truth. "Denial" is the opposite meaning.

8.   **Which of the following words is a synonym of "permissiveness"?**
(Rigorous) (Skill 1.2)

   A.   narrow-mindedness
   B.   intolerance
   C.   tolerance
   D.   insularity

Answer: C. tolerance

A synonym is a different word with a similar meaning. "Permissiveness" allows a certain freedom of behavior. The word with a similar meaning is "tolerance," which is to tolerate, accept, or put up with behavior. All the other choice are antonyms.

9.   **What is the main idea of this passage?**
(Average Rigor) (Skill 2.1)

   A.   Different people have different ideas of what discipline is.
   B.   Permissiveness is the most widely used disciplinary style.
   C.   Most people agree on their definition of discipline.
   D.   There are four disciplinary styles.

Answer: A. Different people have different ideas of what discipline is.

The correct answer is A. Choice C is not true, as the opposite is stated in the passage. Choice B could be true, but we have no evidence of this. Choice D is just one of the many facts listed in the passage.

11. **Consider the following sentence:**

There are four types of disciplinary styles.

What type of sentence is it?
(Rigorous) (Skill 2.3)

A. Summary statement
B. Explanatory statement
C. Supporting statement
D. Introductory statement

Answer: D. Introductory statement

A summary statement summarizes information previously presented in the passage. An explanatory statement explains or clarifies information, while a supporting statement further supports or exemplifies a topic or idea. The introductory statement cues the reader to watch for specific information, as in this case, the four types of disciplinary styles.

11. **Name the four types of disciplinary styles.**
    (Easy) (Skill 3.1)

A. Reasoning, power assertion, morality, and permissiveness.
B. Morality, reasoning, permissiveness, and withdrawal of love.
C. Withdrawal of love, permissiveness, assertion of power, and reasoning.
D. Permissiveness, morality, reasoning, and power assertion.

Answer: C. Withdrawal of love, permissiveness, assertion of power, and reasoning.

These are simply stated in the text. The reader refers to the text to identify these.

12. Consider the following statement from the passage:

"Disciplinary practices have been found to affect diverse areas of child development such as the acquisition of moral values, obedience to authority, and performance at school."

Which statement best reflects the author's attitude toward a possible cause-effect relationship between child development and discipline? *(Rigorous) (Skill 3.3)*

   A. There is no relationship between discipline and child development.
   B. Disciplinary practices explain child behavior.
   C. Child development is impacted by disciplinary practices.
   D. None of these.

Answer: C. Child development is impacted by disciplinary practices.

Option C shows the cause-effect relationship that the author believes exists between child development and disciplinary practices.

13. The author states that "assertion of power involves the use of force to discourage unwanted behavior." Is this a fact or an opinion? *(Average Rigor) (Skill 4.3)*

   A. Fact
   B. Opinion

Answer: A. Fact

The author appears to have done extensive research on this subject. The author simply defines "assertion of power."

DIRECTIONS: Read the following passage and answer the questions that follow.

One of the most difficult problems plaguing American education is the assessment of teachers. No one denies that teachers ought to be answerable for what they do, but what exactly does that mean? The Oxford American Dictionary defines accountability as: the obligation to give a reckoning or explanation for one's actions.

Does a student have to learn for teaching to have taken place? Historically, teaching has not been defined in this restrictive manner; the teacher was thought to be responsible for the quantity and quality of material covered and the way in which it was presented. However, some definitions of teaching now imply that students must learn in order for teaching to have taken place.

As a teacher who tries my best to keep current on all the latest teaching strategies, I believe that those teachers who do not bother even to pick up an educational journal every once in a while should be kept under close watch. There are many teachers out there who have been teaching for decades and refuse to change their ways even if research has proven that their methods are outdated and ineffective. There is no place in the profession of teaching for these types of individuals. It is time that the American educational system clean house, for the sake of our children.

14.   **What is meant by the word "plaguing" in the first sentence? (Easy) (Skill 1.1)**

   A.   Causing problems
   B.   Causing illness
   C.   Causing anger
   D.   Causing failure

Answer: A. Causing problems

The correct answer is A. The first paragraph makes this definition clear.

15. **What is the meaning of the word "reckoning" in the third sentence?**
(Average Rigor) (Skill 1.1)

    A.   Thought
    B.   Answer
    C.   Obligation
    D.   Explanation

Answer: D. Explanation

This is meaning of this word is directly stated in the same sentence.

16. **Which word is an antonym of "bountiful"?**
(Average Rigor) (Skill 1.2)

    A.   profuse
    B.   abundant
    C.   copious
    D.   scarce

Answer: D. scarce

An antonym is a word that means the opposite of the first word. "Scarce" means "insufficient or rarely occurring," so it is the opposite of "bountiful."

17. **What is the main idea of the passage?**
(Average Rigor) (Skill 2.1)

    A.   Teachers should not be answerable for what they do.
    B.   Teachers who do not do their job should be fired.
    C.   The author is a good teacher.
    D.   Assessment of teachers is a serious problem in society today.

Answer: D. Assessment of teachers is a serious problem in society today.

The correct answer is D. The author appears concerned with the assessment of teachers and that teacher quality may affect the quality of education students receive.

18. **Which of the following statements is the topic sentence for paragraph three?**
    (Easy) (Skill 2.2)

    A. As a teacher who tries my best to keep current on all the latest teaching strategies, I believe that those teachers who do not bother even to pick up an educational journal every once in a while should be kept under close watch.
    B. There are many teachers out there who have been teaching for decades and refuse to change their ways even if research has proven that their methods are outdated and ineffective.
    C. There is no place in the profession of teaching for these types of individuals.
    D. It is time that the American educational system clean house, for the sake of our children.

Answer: A. As a teacher who tries my best to keep current on all the latest teaching strategies, I believe that those teachers who do not bother even to pick up an educational journal every once in a while should be kept under close watch.

This statement reveals the author's opinion about other teachers' lackadaisical approach to new or improved teaching methods. At the beginning of the paragraph, it functions as a topic sentence, while others are supporting sentences.

19. **Which of the following sentences is the best summary statement for this passage?**
(Rigorous) (Skill 2.2)

   A. One of the most difficult problems plaguing American education is the assessment of teachers.
   B. However, some definitions of teaching now imply that students must learn in order for teaching to have taken place.
   C. It is time that the American educational system clean house, for the sake of our children.

Answer: C. It is time that the American educational system clean house, for the sake of our children.

The summary statement, found at or near the end of the passage, sums up the author's main point. Here, the author's emotional plea for change is summarizes the opinions presented throughout the passage.

20. **The author states that teacher assessment is a problem for**
(Easy) (Skill 2.3)

   A. Elementary schools
   B. Secondary schools
   C. American education
   D. Families

Answer: C. American education

The author identifies teacher assessment as a problem and spends the rest of the passage defining why it is considered a problem.

21. Teachers who do not keep current on educational trends should be fired. Is this a fact or an opinion?
     (Average Rigor) (Skill 4.3)

     A. Fact
     B. Opinion

Answer: B. Opinion

The words "should be" imply that if one condition isn't met, something else should happen as a result. This is an opinion statement. In addition, there may be those who feel they can be good teachers by using old methods.

DIRECTIONS: Read the following passage and answer the questions that follow.

Mr. Smith gave instructions for the painting to be hung on the wall. And then it leaped forth before his eyes: the little cottages on the river, the white clouds floating over the valley and the green of the towering mountain ranges which were seen in the distance. The painting was so vivid that it seemed almost real. Mr. Smith was now absolutely certain that the painting had been the worth the money.

22. **What is the meaning of the word "vivid" in the third sentence?**
   (Average Rigor) (Skill 1.1)

   A. Lifelike
   B. Dark
   C. Expensive
   D. Big

Answer: A. Lifelike

This is reinforced by the second half of the same sentence.

23. **What does the author mean by the expression "it leaped forth before his eyes"?**
   (Rigorous) (Skill 1.1)

   A. The painting fell off the wall.
   B. The painting appeared so real it was almost three-dimensional.
   C. The painting struck Mr. Smith in the face.
   D. Mr. Smith was hallucinating.

Answer: B. The painting appeared so real it was almost three-dimensional.

This is almost directly stated in the third sentence.

24.   **What is the main idea of this passage?**
       (Average Rigor) (Skill 2.1)

   A.   The painting that Mr. Smith purchased is expensive.
   B.   Mr. Smith purchased a painting.
   C.   Mr. Smith was pleased with the quality of the painting he had purchased.
   D.   The painting depicted cottages and valleys.

Answer: C. Mr. Smith was please with the quality of the painting he had purchased.

Every sentence in the paragraph alludes to this fact.

25.   **Select the correct word to complete the sentence correctly.**
       (Rigorous) (Skill 1.3)

       He _____ her backpack down near the bin filled with shoes.

   A.   sat
   B.   set
   C.   sets

Answer: B. set

Use the transitive verb "set," meaning "to put or to place." "Sit" is an intransitive verb meaning "to be seated," and "sat" is the past tense form.

28. **Select the correct combination of words to complete the sentence correctly.**
(Rigorous) (Skill 1.3)

_____ you and me, our grandfather cannot tell the difference _____ those triplets.

A. Between, between
B. Between, amongst
C. Between, among

Answer: C. Between, among

Use "between" with two items; use "among" as a preposition for three or more items.

29. **Select the correct word to complete the sentence correctly.**
(Rigorous) (Skill 1.3)

The move from Idaho to Chicago _____ the young boy in many ways.

A. affected
B. effects
C. effected

Answer: C. effected

Use the noun, effect, when speaking about an outcome. "Affect" is a verb, an action that produces the effect.

28.   Organize the following set of instructions into its proper sequence. *(Average Rigor) (Skill 3.2)*

    1. Pick up the knife, dip it into the peanut butter, and spread it on one slice of bread.

    2. Press the two pieces together and serve.

    3. On the other slice of bread, spread your favorite jelly.

    4. Put the spoon down.

    5. Remove two pieces of bread from the bag and set them on the counter.

    6. Put the knife down.

    7. Open the jelly and pick up the spoon.

    A. 7, 3, 2, 1, 6, 2, 4

    B. 5, 7, 3, 1, 6, 4, 2

    C. 5, 1, 6, 7, 3, 4, 2

Answer: C. 5, 1, 6, 7, 3, 4, 2

The correct answer must start with five because removing the two pieces of bread has to happen first, so this rules out Option A. Option B is incorrect because the spoon is picked up and used in number 7, and then not put down until number 4.

29.   Organize the following set of instructions into its proper sequence. *(Rigorous) (Skill 3.2)*

1.   Remove the spare tire from its location, obtain the jack, and lug wrench.

2.   Pry off the flat tire's hubcap using the sharp end of the lug wrench, a screwdriver, or a utility knife.

3.   Place the car in "park" and apply the parking brake.

4.   To loosen each lug nut, turn the wrench counterclockwise about one turn while the tire is still on the ground.

5.   Finally, use the wrench to tighten each lug nut tightly.

6.   Jack up the car until the flat tire is several inches off the ground, providing enough clearance to remove the tire.

7.   Remove the lug nuts and remove the wheel.

8.   Pull safely off the road.

9.   Replace the lug nuts and tighten each lightly.

10. Lower the car to the ground and remove the jack.

11. Lift the spare tire onto the axle hub and align the holes.

12. Place the jack under the reinforced section of the car's body.

A. 3, 1, 2, 4, 6, 7, 11, 12, 8, 9, 10, 5

B. 8, 3, 1, 2, 4, 12, 6, 7, 11, 9, 10, 5

C. 8, 1, 3, 12, 6, 2, 7, 4, 11, 10, 9, 5

Answer: B. 8, 3, 1, 2, 4, 12, 6, 7, 11, 9, 10, 5

Option A is incorrect because the car must be pulled over and stopped (number 8) before applying the parking brake (number 3).

30.   Consider the data in the bar graph below. Which of the following
       statements is true?
       (Average Rigor) (Skill 4.1)

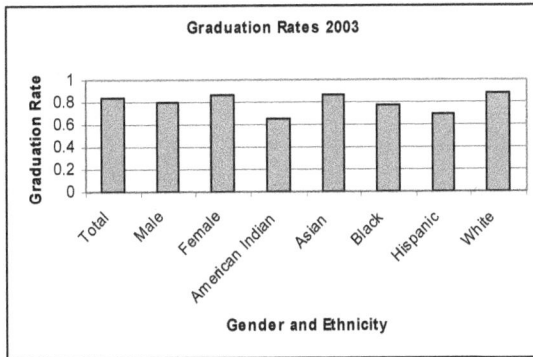

Graduation Rates 2003

A. More males graduated in 2003 than females.

B. In 2003, American Indian and Black students held the lowest
    graduation rate.

C. Based on this information, one could infer that Hispanics had the
    highest dropout rate.

D. Female, Asian, and white students had the highest graduation
    rates.

**Answer: D. Female, Asian, and white students had the highest graduation
             rates.**

Option A is incorrect because the bars show more females than males graduating.
Otpion B is incorrect because American Indian and Hispanic students had the lowest
graduation rate. Based on the bar graph one could infer that American Indians *or*
Hispanics had the highest dropout rate, but Option D is correct because the bars
clearly show females, Asians, and white students with graduation rates higher than the
others.

31. Consider the data in the bar graph below. Which of the following
    statements is *not* true?
    (Rigorous) (Skill 4.1)

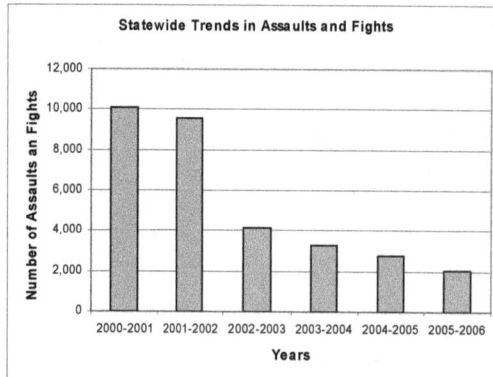

A. One could infer that anti-bullying programs in K-12 schools helped decrease physical violence.

B. Over the six-year period, the number of assaults or fights decreased by about 40%.

C. Over the six-year period, the number of assaults or fights decreased by about 80%.

D. The 2002-2003 school year showed a sharp decline in physical violence.

Answer: B. **Over the six-year period, the number of assaults or fights decreased by about 40%.**

The number of assaults actually decreased by about 80% (10,000 to 2,000). All statements are true except for B.

32. Consider the data in the pie chart below. Which of the following is *not* true?
(*Rigorous*) (*Skill 4.1*)

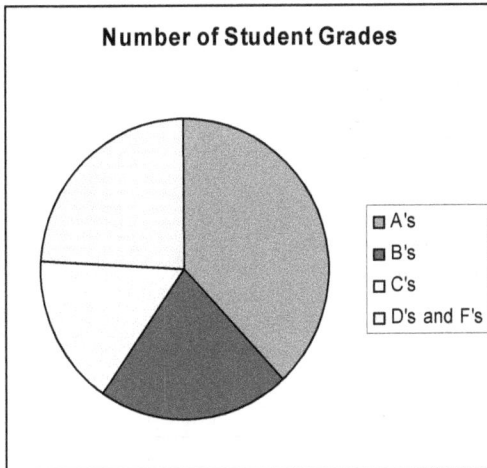

Number of Student Grades

- A's
- B's
- C's
- D's and F's

A. Nearly 1/3 of these students received a B or a C.

B. Nearly 30% of this teacher's students failed this grading period.

C. This teacher may need to challenge high-achieving students more.

D. This teacher may need to find ways to motivate underachieving students.

Answer: B. Nearly 30% of this teacher's students failed this grading period.

Option B is the only statement that is not true because the amount of failing students is just under 25%, or ¼ of the pie. A is true, as the B's and C's equal 1/3 of the pie when added together. Due to the high number of students receiving A's, this teacher may need to make sure all students are challenged appropriately. Due to the high number of D's and F's, this teacher may need to motivate underachieving students to achieve better grades.

33. The following is a set of data from a class of students who completed a survey on learning styles and strengths. Which bar graph shows the correct data for this class?
(Average Rigor) (Skill 4.2)

Section	Total
I	2
II	4
III	8
IV	7
V	3
VI	6
VII	0
VIII	1

Bar Graph A

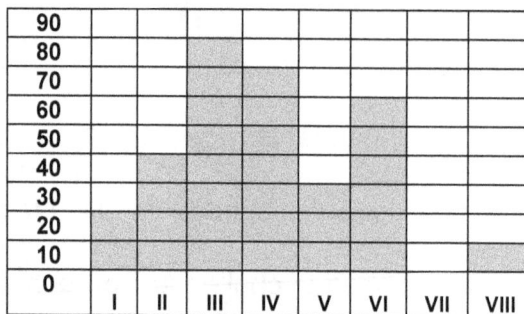

Bar Graph B

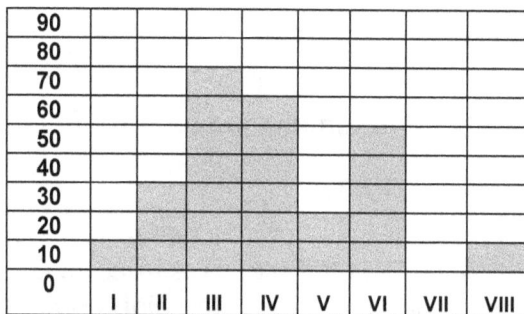

Bar Graph C

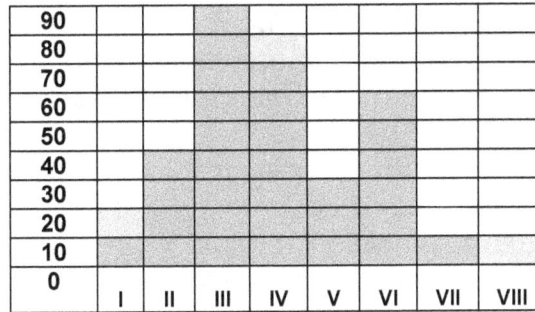

 A. Bar Graph A

 B. Bar Graph B

 C. Bar Graph C

Answer: A. Bar Graph A

Bar Graph A shows the correct amounts for each category. Graph B is short by one unit in all categories except the eighth. Graph C does not match any of the class's data.

35.   **Which of the following statements is an opinion?**
        (Easy) (Skill 4.3)

        A. Frogs are amphibians.

        B. When fall weather turns cold, it's best to dress in layers.

        C. Blue and yellow make green.

        D. Her living room décor seems ancient.

Answer: D. Her living room décor seems ancient.

The word "seems" signals an opinion statement. Option B is common advice supported by research.

DIRECTIONS : *The passage below contains many errors. Read the passage. Then answer each test item by choosing the option that corrects an error in the underlined portion(s). No more than one underlined error will appear in each item. If no error exists, choose "No change is necessary."*

Climbing to the top of Mount Everest is an adventure. One which everyone-- whether physically fit or not--seems eager to try. The trail stretches for miles, the cold temperatures are usually frigid and brutal.

Climbers must endure severel barriers on the way, including other hikers, steep jagged rocks, and lots of snow. Plus, climbers often find the most grueling part of the trip is their climb back down, just when they are feeling greatly exhausted. Climbers who take precautions are likely to find the ascent less arduous than the unprepared. By donning heavy flannel shirts, gloves, and hats, climbers prevented hypothermia, as well as simple frostbite. A pair of rugged boots is also one of the necesities. If climbers are to avoid becoming dehydrated, there is beverages available for them to transport as well.

Once climbers are completely ready to begin there lengthy journey, they can comfortably enjoy the wonderful scenery. Wide rock formations dazzle the observers eyes with shades of gray and white, while the peak forms a triangle that seems to touch the sky. Each of the climbers are reminded of the splendor and magnifisence of Gods great Earth.

35. **Each of the climbers <u>are</u> reminded of the splendor and <u>magnifisence</u> of <u>God's</u> great Earth.**
    (Rigorous) (Skill 5.1)

    A. is
    B. magnifisence
    C. Gods
    D. No change is necessary

Answer: A. is

The singular verb *is* agrees with the singular subject *each.* Option B is incorrect because *magnificence* is misspelled. Option C is incorrect because an apostrophe is needed to show possession.

36. **Plus, climbers often find the most grueling part of the trip is <u>their</u> climb back <u>down, just</u> when they <u>are</u> feeling greatly exhausted.**
(Average Rigor) (Skill 5.2)

   A. his
   B. down; just
   C. were
   D. No change is necessary

Answer: D. No change is necessary

The present tense must be used consistently throughout, therefore Option C is incorrect. Option A is incorrect because the singular pronoun *his* does not agree with the plural antecedent *climbers*. Option B is incorrect because a comma, not a semicolon, is needed to separate the dependent clause from the main clause.

37. **Once climbers are completely prepared for <u>there</u> lengthy <u>journey, they</u> can comfortably enjoy the <u>wonderful</u> scenery.**
(Average Rigor) (Skill 6.2)

   A. wonderfull
   B. journey; they
   C. their
   D. No change is necessary

Answer: C. their

The possessive pronoun *their* must be used and spelled correctly. Option A is misspelled. Option B is incorrect because a semi-colon would make the first half of the item seem like an independent clause when the subordinating conjunction *once* makes that clause dependent.

38. **Climbers who** take precautions are likely to find the ascent **less difficult than** the unprepared.
     (Average Rigor) (Skill 6.3)

     A. Climbers, who
     B. least difficult
     C. then
     D. No change is necessary

Answer: D. No change is necessary

No change is needed. Option A is incorrect because a comma would make the restrictive or less essential to the sentence. Option B is incorrect because *less* is appropriate when two items--the prepared and the unprepared--are compared. Option C is incorrect because the comparative adverb *than*, not *then*, is needed.

39. **Climbing to the top of Mount Everest is an adventure. One** which everyone **—whether** physically fit or not—**seems** eager to try.
     (Rigorous) (Skill 7.3)

     A. adventure, one
     B. people, whether
     C. seem
     D. No change is necessary

Answer: A. adventure, one

A comma is needed between *adventure* and *one* to avoid creating a fragment of the second part. In Option B, a comma after *everyone* would not be appropriate when the dash is used on the other side of *not*. In Option C, the singular verb *seems* is needed to agree with the singular subject *everyone*.

40. The <u>trail</u> stretches for <u>miles</u>, the cold temperatures are <u>usually</u> frigid and brutal.
    (Rigorous) (Skill 7.3)

    A. trails
    B. miles;
    C. usual
    D. No change is necessary

Answer: B. miles;

A semicolon, not a comma, is needed to separate the first independent clause from the second independent clause. Option A is incorrect because the plural subject *trails* needs the singular verb stretch. Option C is incorrect because the adverb form *usually* is needed to modify the adjective *frigid.*

41. Climbers must endure <u>severel</u> barriers <u>on the way, including</u> other <u>hikers</u>, steep jagged rocks, and lots of snow.
    (Easy) (Skill 8.3)

    A. several
    B. on the way: including
    C. hikers'
    D. No change is necessary

Answer: A. several

The word *several* is misspelled in the text. Option B is incorrect because a comma, not a colon, is needed to set off the modifying phrase. Option C is incorrect because no apostrophe is needed after *hikers* since possession is not involved.

42.   **A pair of rugged boots <u>is</u> <u>also one</u> of the <u>necesities</u>.**
      (Rigorous) (Skill 8.3)

   A. are
   B. also, one
   C. necessities
   D. No change is necessary

Answer: C. necessities

The word *necessities* is misspelled in the text. Option A is incorrect because the singular verb is must agree with the singular noun *pair* (a collective singular). Option B is incorrect because *if also* is set off with commas (potential correction), it should be set off on both sides.

DIRECTIONS: *The passage below contains several errors. Read the passage. Then answer each test item by choosing the option that corrects an error in the underlined portion(s). No more than one underlined error will appear in each item. If no error exists, choose "No change is necessary."*

Every job places different kinds of demands on their employees. For example, whereas such jobs as accounting and bookkeeping require mathematical ability; graphic design requires creative/artistic ability.

Doing good at one job does not usually guarantee success at another. However, one of the elements crucial to all jobs are especially notable: the chance to accomplish a goal.

The accomplishment of the employees varies according to the job. In many jobs the employees become accustom to the accomplishment provided by the work they do every day.

In medicine, for example, every doctor tests him self by treating badly injured or critically ill people. In the operating room, a team of Surgeons is responsible for operating on many of these patients. In addition to the feeling of accomplishment that the workers achieve, some jobs also give a sense of identity to the employees'. Profesions like law, education, and sales offer huge financial and emotional rewards. Politicians are public servants: who work for the federal and state governments. President bush is basically employed by the American people to make laws and run the country.

Finally; the contributions that employees make to their companies and to the world cannot be taken for granted. Through their work, employees are performing a service for their employers and are contributing something to the world.

43. <u>However,</u> one of the elements crucial to all jobs <u>are</u> especially <u>notable:</u> the accomplishment of a goal.
    (Rigorous) (Skill 5.1)

   A. However
   B. is
   C. notable;
   D. No change is necessary

Answer: B. is

The singular verb *is* is needed to agree with the singular subject *one.* Option A is incorrect because a comma is needed to set off the transitional word *however.* Option C is incorrect because a colon, not a semicolon, is needed to set off an item.

44. The <u>accomplishment</u> of the <u>employees</u> <u>varies</u> according to the job.
     (Rigorous) (Skill 5.1)

     A. accomplishment,
     B. employee's
     C. vary
     D. No change is necessary

Answer: C. vary

The singular verb *vary* is needed to agree with the singular subject
accomplishment. Option A is incorrect because a comma after *accomplishment*
would suggest that the modifying phrase of the employees is additional instead of
essential. Option B is incorrect because employees is not possessive.

45. In many jobs the employees <u>become</u> <u>accustom</u> to the accomplishment
     <u>provided</u> by the work they do every day.
     (Average Rigor) (Skill 5.2)

     A. became
     B. accustomed
     C. provides
     D. No change is necessary

Answer: B. accustomed

The past participle *accustomed* is needed with the verb *become*. Option A is
incorrect because the verb tense does not need to change to the past *became*.
Option C is incorrect because *provides* is the wrong tense.

46. In medicine, for example, every doctor <u>tests</u> <u>him self</u> by treating badly injured and critically ill people.
(Average Rigor) (Skill 6.1)

    A. test
    B. himself
    C. critical
    D. No change is necessary

Answer: B. himself

The reflexive pronoun *himself* is needed. (Him self is nonstandard and never correct.) Option A is incorrect because the singular verb test is needed to agree with the singular subject doctor. Option C is incorrect because the adverb *critically* is needed to modify the verb *ill*.

47. Every job <u>places</u> different kinds of demands on <u>their</u> <u>employees</u>.
(Rigorous) (Skill 6.2)

    A. place
    B. its
    C. employes
    D. No change is necessary

Answer: B. its

The singular possessive pronoun *its* must agree with its antecedent *job*, which is singular also. Option A is incorrect because *place* is a plural form and the subject, *job*, is singular. Option C is incorrect because the correct spelling of employees is given in the sentence.

48. Doing <u>good</u> at one job does not <u>usually</u> guarantee <u>success</u> at another.
    (Rigorous) (Skill 6.3)

    A. well
    B. usualy
    C. succeeding
    D. No change is necessary

Answer: A. well

The adverb *well* modifies the word *doing*. Option B is incorrect because *usually* is spelled correctly in the sentence. Option C is incorrect because *succeeding* is in the wrong tense.

49. Politicians <u>are</u> public <u>servants: who</u> <u>work</u> for the federal and state governments.
    (Easy) (Skill 7.3)

    A. were
    B. servants who
    C. worked
    D. No change is necessary

Answer: B. servants who

A colon is not needed to set off the introduction of the sentence. In Option A, *were*, is the incorrect tense of the verb. In Option C, *worked*, is in the wrong tense.

50. <u>For example, whereas</u> such jobs as accounting and bookkeeping require mathematical <u>ability;</u> graphic design requires creative/artistic ability.
(Average Rigor) (Skill 7.3)

    A. For example
    B. whereas,
    C. ability,
    D. No change is necessary

Answer: C. ability,

An introductory dependent clause is set off with a comma, not a semicolon. Option A is incorrect because the transitional phrase *for example* should be set off with a comma. Option B is incorrect because the adverb *whereas* functions like *while* and does not take a comma after it.

51. In addition to the feeling of accomplishment that the workers <u>achieve</u>, some jobs also <u>give</u> a sense of self-identity to the <u>employees'.</u>
(Average Rigor) (Skill 7.3)

    A. acheive
    B. gave
    C. employees
    D. No change is necessary

Answer: C. employees

Option C is correct because *employees* is not possessive. Option A is incorrect because *achieve* is spelled correctly in the sentence. Option B is incorrect because *gave* is the wrong tense.

52. **Finally; the contributions that employees make to their companies and to the world cannot be taken for granted.**
(Average Rigor) (Skill 7.3)

A. Finally,
B. their
C. took
D. No change is necessary

Answer: A. Finally,

A comma is needed to separate *Finally* from the rest of the sentence. Finally is a preposition, which usually heads a dependent sentence, hence a comma is needed. Option B is incorrect because *their* is misspelled. Option C is incorrect because *took* is the wrong form of the verb.

53. **In the operating room, a team of Surgeons is responsible for operating on many of these patients.**
(Easy) (Skill 8.2)

A. operating room:
B. surgeons is
C. those
D. No change is necessary

Answer: B. surgeons is

Surgeons is not a proper name so it does not need to be capitalized. A comma is not needed to break up a team of surgeons from the rest of the sentence. Option A is incorrect because a comma ,not a colon, is needed to set off an item. Option C is incorrect because *those* is an incorrect pronoun.

54. **President bush is basically employed <u>by</u> the American people to <u>make</u> laws and run the country.**
   (Easy) (Skill 8.2)

   A. Bush
   B. to
   C. made
   D. No change is necessary

Answer: A. Bush

Bush is a proper name and should be capitalized. Option B, *to*, does not fit with the verb *employed*. Option C uses the wrong form of the verb, *make*.

55. **<u>Profesions</u> like law, <u>education,</u> and sales <u>offer</u> huge financial and emotional rewards.**
   (Average Rigor) (Skill 8.3)

   A. Professions
   B. education;
   C. offered
   D. No change is necessary

Answer: A. Professions

Option A is correct because *professions* is misspelled in the sentence. Option B is incorrect because a comma, not a semi-colon, is needed after *education*. In Option C, *offered*, is in the wrong tense.

56. **Choose the sentence that demonstrates correct verb tense.**
(Average Rigor) (Skill 5.2)

A. He should have went to the store last night.

B. He should of went to the store last night.

C. He should of gone to the store last night.

D. He should have gone to the store last night.

Answer: D. He should have gone to the store last night.

The past participle of the verb *to go* is *gone*. *Went* is incorrect because is expresses the simple past tense. *Should of* is a nonstandard expression, and *of* is not a verb. *Should of* and *should have* are commonly mistaken, especially when spoken orally.

57. **Choose the sentence that logically and correctly expresses the comparison.**
(Easy) (Skill 6.3)

A. The Empire State Building in New York is taller than buildings in the city.

B. The Empire State Building in New York is taller than any other building in the city.

C. The Empire State Building in New York is tallest than other buildings in the city.

Answer: B. The Empire State Building in New York is taller than any other building in the city.

Because the Empire State Building is a building in New York City, the phrase *any other* must be included. Option A is incorrect because the Empire State Building is implicitly compared to itself since it is one of the buildings. Option C is incorrect because *tallest* is the incorrect form of the adjective.

58.   **Identify the complete sentence below.**
       (Average Rigor) (Skill 7.1)

   A. The pastor waiting for the offering basket to be passed through the crowd.

   B. Growling at the back door as her owner hoped the cat would leave.

   C. He didn't finish mowing the lawn, so he couldn't attend the birthday party.

   D. By paying too much attention to interest surveys can make a teacher unaware of students' academic needs.

Answer: C.   He didn't finish mowing the lawn, so he couldn't attend the birthday party.

Option C is the only sentence that contains a subject and a verb. Its two clauses are joined correctly by a comma and conjunction, *so*.

59.   **Choose the sentence that is complete and written correctly.**
       (Rigorous) (Skill 7.1)

   A. Even though there are a number of different methods for helping the patient overcome a dependency.

   B. Even though different methods can help a patient overcome a dependency, there is no way to know which is best in the long-run.

   C. Even though there is no way to know which way is best patients can overcome their dependencies when they are helped.

   D. None of these sentences is correct.

Answer: B.   Even though different methods can help a patient overcome a dependency, there is no way to know which is best in the long-run.

Option A is a fragment. Option C is missing the correct comma punctuation.

60.   Choose the sentence that is complete and written correctly.
       (Rigorous) (Skill 7.2)

   A. There are too many or too few qualified candidates for a certain
       position, and then they have to be confirmed by the Senate where
       there is the possibility of rejection.

   B. Either there are too many or too few qualified candidate for a certain
       position then they have to be confirmed by the Senate, where there is
       the possibility of rejection.

   C. The Senate has to confirm qualified candidates, who face the
       possibility of rejection.

   D. Because the Senate has to confirm qualified candidates; they face the
       possibility of rejection.

**Answer: C.   The Senate has to confirm qualified candidates, who face the
             possibility of rejection.**

Option A is a run-on sentence and does not have any comma punctuation.
Option B is also a run-on, missing the comma and conjunction *and*. Option D is
incorrect because it should have a comma instead of a semi-colon to join the two
clauses.

61.   A run-on sentence is listed below. Choose the item that shows the
       correct sentence structure.
       (Rigorous) (Skill 7.2)

   I made the cookies I didn't clean up the kitchen.

   A. I made the cookies, but I didn't clean up the kitchen.

   B. After I made the cookies I didn't clean up the kitchen.

   C. I didn't clean up the kitchen, I made the cookies.

Answer: A.   I made the cookies, but I didn't clean up the kitchen.

Option A fixes the run-on sentence by joining the two clauses with a comma and
conjunction, *but*. Option B needs a comma and Option C needs a conjunction or a
preposition without a comma in order to be correct.

62. **Choose the sentence that is complete and written correctly.** *(Rigorous) (Skill 7.3)*

   A. Overcrowding budget cutbacks and societal deterioration have greatly affected student learning.

   B. Student learning has been greatly affected by overcrowding, budget cutbacks, and societal deterioration.

   C. Due to overcrowding, budget cutbacks, and societal deterioration student learning has been greatly affected.

   D. None of these sentences is correct.

Answer: B. Student learning has been greatly affected by overcrowding, budget cutbacks, and societal deterioration.

Using commas correctly in a list – Option A is missing all commas. Option C needs a comma after *deterioration*.

63. **Select the underline section that is capitalized correctly.**

   the bombing of the Oklahoma City Federal Building was considered to be one of the worst Terrorist incidents on American Soil *(Easy) (Skill 8.2)*

   A. the bombing

   B. Oklahoma City Federal Building

   C. Terrorist

   D. American Soil

Answer: B.   Oklahoma City Federal Building

At the beginning of the sentence, *the* should be capitalized. *Terrorist* is not a proper noun, thus it should not be capitalized. *American* should be capitalized because it is a proper noun, but *soil* should not be capitalized.

64. **Select the underline section that is capitalized correctly.**

The **Flu** epidemic struck most of the respected faculty and students of the Woolbright School, forcing the Boynton Beach School Superintendent to close it down for two weeks.
(Average Rigor) (Skill 8.2)

A. Flu

B. the Woolbright School

C. Boynton Beach School Superintendent

D. None of these is capitalized correctly.

Answer: C. Boynton Beach School Superintendent

Flu is not a proper noun and should not be capitalized. In Option B, *the* should be capitalized because it is part of the school's name, which makes it part of the proper noun.

65. **Round $1\dfrac{13}{16}$ of an inch to the nearest quarter of an inch.**
(Average Rigor) (Skill 9.2)

A. $1\dfrac{1}{4}$ inch

B. $1\dfrac{5}{8}$ inch

C. $1\dfrac{3}{4}$ inch

D.   2 inches

Answer: C. $1\dfrac{3}{4}$ inch

$1\dfrac{13}{16}$ inches is approximately $1\dfrac{12}{16}$, which is also $1\dfrac{3}{4}$, which is the nearest $\dfrac{1}{4}$ of an inch.

66. **What unit of measurement could we use to report the distance traveled walking around a track?**
    (Easy) (Skill 9.3)

    A. degrees

    B. square meters

    C. kilometers

    D. cubic feet

Answer: C. kilometers

Degrees measures angles, square meters measures area, cubic feet measure volume, and kilometers measures length. Kilometers is the only reasonable answer.

67. **What unit of measurement would describe the spread of a forest fire in a unit time?**
    (Average Rigor) (Skill 9.3)

    A. 10 square yards per second

    B. 10 yards per minute

    C. 10 feet per hour

    D. 10 cubit feet per hour

Answer: A. 10 square yards per second

The only appropriate answer is one that describes "an area" of forest consumed per unit time. All answers are not units of area measurement except answer A.

68. **3 km is equivalent to**
(Average Rigor) (Skill 9.3)

A. 300 cm

B. 300 m

C. 3000 cm

D. 3000 m

Answer: D. 3000 m

To change kilometers to meters, move the decimal 3 places to the right.

69. **The mass of a cookie is closest to:**
(Rigorous) (Skill 9.3)

A. 0.5 kg

B. 0.5 grams

C. 15 grams

D. 1.5 grams

Answer: C. 15 grams

28 grams equal an ounce, and 16 ounces equal a pound. Option A, 0.5 kg is equal to 500 grams, which is just over a pound. Options B and D are too light.

70. The following chart shows the yearly average number of international tourists visiting Palm Beach for 1990-1994. How many more international tourists visited Palm Beach in 1994 than in 1991? *(Average Rigor) (Skill 10.2)*

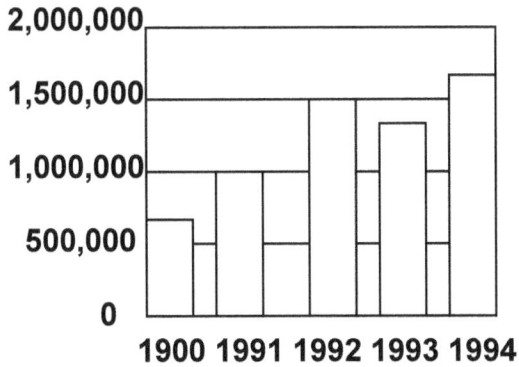

    A.   100,000

    B.   600,000

    C.   1,600,000

    D.   8,000,000

Answer: B. 600,000

The number of tourists in 1991 was 1,000,000 and the number in 1994 was 1,600,000. Subtract to get a difference of 600,000.

71.   (576 + 29) – (52 – 27) =
       (Easy) (Skill 10.3)

    A.   580

    B.   526

    C.   680

    D.   589

Answer: A. 580

Use order of operations and complete the parentheses first:

```
  1 1
  576
+  29
  605

  52
-  27
  25

 5 10
 6̶05
 - 25
 580
```

72. **1250 ÷ 50 =**
    (Easy) (Skill 11.2)

     A.   20
     B.   25
     C.   15
     D.   40

Answer: B. 25

$$50\overline{)1250}$$

$$\begin{array}{r} 2 \\ 50\overline{)1250} \end{array}$$

$$\begin{array}{r} 2 \\ 50\overline{)1250} \\ -100 \\ \hline 250 \end{array}$$

$$\begin{array}{r} 25 \\ 50\overline{)1250} \\ -100 \\ \hline 250 \\ -250 \\ \hline 0 \end{array}$$

73. **A sofa sells for $520. If the retailer makes a 30% profit, what was the wholesale price?**
    (Rigorous) (Skill 11.3)

     A. $400
     B. $676
     C. $490
     D. $364

Answer: A. $400

Let x be the wholesale price, then $x + .30x = 520$, $1.30x = 520$. Divide both sides by 1.30.

74. The price of gas was $3.27 per gallon. Your tank holds 15 gallons of fuel. You are using two tanks a week. How much will you save weekly if the price of gas goes down to $2.30 per gallon?
(Average Rigor) (Skill 11.3)

    A. $26.00

    B. $29.00

    C. $15.00

    D. $17.00

Answer: B. $29.00

15 gallons x 2 tanks = 30 gallons a week
= 30 gallons x $3.27 = $98.10
30 gallons x $2.30 = $69.00
$98.10 - $69.00 = $29.10 is approximately $29.00.

75. Two mathematics classes have a total of 410 students. The 8:00 am class has 40 more than the 10:00 am class. How many students are in the 10:00 am class?
(Rigorous) (Skill 11.3)

    A.   123.3

    B.   370

    C.   185

    D.   330

Answer: C. 185

Let x = # of students in the 8 am class and $x - 40$ = # of students in the 10 am class. $x + (x - 40) = 410 \rightarrow 2x - 40 = 410 \rightarrow 2x = 450 \rightarrow x = 225$. So there are 225 students in the 8 am class, and $225 - 40 = 185$ in the 10 am class.

76. If $4x - (3 - x) = 7(x - 3) + 10$, then
   (Rigorous) (Skill 11.3)

   A. $x = 8$

   B. $x = -8$

   C. $x = 4$

   D. $x = -4$

Answer: C. x = 4

Solve for x.

$$4x - (3 - x) = 7(x - 3) + 10$$
$$4x - 3 + x = 7x - 21 + 10$$
$$5x - 3 = 7x - 11$$
$$5x = 7x - 11 + 3$$
$$5x - 7x = {}^{-}8$$
$${}^{-}2x = {}^{-}8$$
$$x = 4$$

77. $\dfrac{7}{9} + \dfrac{1}{3} \div \dfrac{2}{3} =$

    (Average Rigor) (Skill 12.1)

    A. $\dfrac{5}{3}$

    B. $\dfrac{3}{2}$

    C. 2

    D. $\dfrac{23}{18}$

Answer: D. $\dfrac{23}{18}$

First, do the division. $\dfrac{1}{3} \div \dfrac{2}{3} = \dfrac{1}{3} \times \dfrac{3}{2} = \dfrac{1}{2}$ Add. $\dfrac{7}{9} + \dfrac{1}{2} = \dfrac{14}{18} + \dfrac{9}{18} = \dfrac{23}{18}$.

78. Which statement is true about George's budget?
(Average Rigor) (Skill 12.1)

A. George spends the greatest portion of his income on food.

B. George spends twice as much on utilities as he does on his mortgage.

C. George spends twice as much on utilities as he does on food.

D. George spends the same amount on food and utilities as he does on his mortgage.

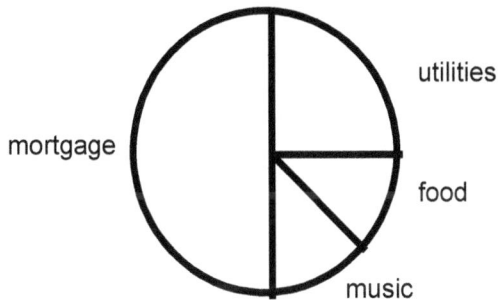

Answer: C. George spends twice as much on utilities as he does on food.

George spends twice as much on utilities as on food, so the answer is C.

79. $\left(\dfrac{^-4}{9}\right) + \left(\dfrac{^-7}{10}\right) =$

(Rigorous) (Skill 12.1)

A. $\dfrac{23}{90}$

B. $\dfrac{^-23}{90}$

C. $\dfrac{103}{90}$

D. $\dfrac{^-103}{90}$

Answer: D. $\dfrac{^-103}{90}$

Find the LCD of $\dfrac{^-4}{9}$ and $\dfrac{^-7}{10}$. The LCD is 90, so you get $\dfrac{^-40}{90} + \dfrac{^-63}{90} = \dfrac{^-103}{90}$.

80. $4\dfrac{2}{9} \times \dfrac{7}{10}$

    (Rigorous) (Skill 12.1)

    A. $4\dfrac{9}{10}$

    B. $\dfrac{266}{90}$

    C. $2\dfrac{43}{45}$

    D. $2\dfrac{6}{20}$

Answer: C. $2\dfrac{43}{45}$

Convert any mixed number to an improper fraction: $\dfrac{38}{9} x \dfrac{7}{10}$. Since no common factors of numerators or denominators exist, multiply the numerators and the denominators by each other = $\dfrac{266}{90}$. Convert back to a mixed number and reduce $2\dfrac{86}{90} = 2\dfrac{43}{45}$.

81. $(5.6) \times (^-0.11) =$

    (Average Rigor) (Skill 12.2)

    A. $^-0.616$

    B. 0.616

    C. $^-6.110$

    D. 6.110

Answer: A. -0.616

Simple multiplication. The answer will be negative because a positive times a negative is a negative number. $5.6 \times ^- 0.11 =^- 0.616$.

82. **An item that sells for $375 is put on sale at $120. What is the percent of decrease?**
    (Rigorous) (Skill 12.3)

    A. 25%

    B. 28%

    C. 68%

    D. 34%

Answer: C. 68%

Use $(1 - x)$ as the discount. $375x = 120$.
$375(1 - x) = 120 \rightarrow 375 - 375x = 120 \rightarrow 375x = 255 \rightarrow x = 0.68 = 68\%$.

83. A movie theater has a 500-person capacity. At the start of a movie, 457 seats were taken. By the end of the movie, 96 people had left early. What was the percent change in occupied seats from the beginning to the end of the movie?
    (Rigorous) (Skill 12.3)

    A.   15%

    B.   17%

    C.   19.2%

    D.   19.7%

Answer: C. 19.2%

Restate the problem: 457 out of 500 seats were taken at the beginning, and 96 were vacated during the movie, leaving 361 people in the theatre (457-96 = 361).

Percent of capacity at the beginning: b = 457/500 = 91.4% seats filled

Percent of capacity at the end: e = 361/500 = 72.2% seats filled

Subtract (b-e) to find the change in capacity: 91.4 – 72.2 = 19.2%

84. **0.74 =**
    (Easy) (Skill 12.4)

    A. $\dfrac{74}{100}$

    B.   7.4%

    C. $\dfrac{33}{50}$

    D. $\dfrac{74}{10}$

Answer: A. $\dfrac{74}{100}$

0.74→the 4 is in the hundredths place, so the answer is $\dfrac{74}{100}$.

85. **303 is what percent of 600?**
    (Easy) (Skill 12.4)

    A.   0.505%

    B.   5.05%

    C.   505%

    D.   50.5%

Answer: D. 50.5%

Use x for the percent. $600x = 303$. $\dfrac{600x}{600} = \dfrac{303}{600} \rightarrow x = 0.505 = 50.5\%$.

86. **Jim must deliver 65% of his campaign flyers by the end of the week. If he has 700 flyers, how many must he deliver to meet this requirement?**
    (Average Rigor) (Skill 12.4)

    A. 475 flyers

    B. 425 flyers

    C. 435 flyers

    D. 455 flyers

Answer: D. 455 flyers

Convert the percentage to decimal and use x for the number of flyers. $(.65)(700) = x$.

87.   A restaurant employs 465 people. There are 280 waiters and 185 cooks. If 168 waiters and 85 cooks receive pay raises, what percent of the waiters will receive a pay raise?
       (Average Rigor) (Skill 12.4)

       A.   36.13%

       B.   60%

       C.   60.22%

       D.   40%

Answer: B. 60%

The total number of waiters is 280 and only 168 of them get a pay raise. Divide the number getting a raise by the total number of waiters to get the percent.
$\dfrac{168}{280} = 0.6 = 60\%$.

88.   Choose the equation that is equivalent to the following:

       $$\dfrac{3x}{5} - 5 = 5x$$
       (Rigorous) (Skill 12.4)

       A. $3x - 25 = 25x$

       B. $x - \dfrac{25}{3} = 25x$

       C. $6x - 50 = 75x$

       D. $x + 25 = 25x$

Answer: A. $3x - 25 = 25x$

A is the correct answer because it is the original equation multiplied by 5. The other choices alter the answer to the original equation.

89.   In a sample of 40 full-time employees at a particular company, 35 were also holding down a part-time   job requiring at least 10 hours/week. If this proportion holds for the entire company of 25000 employees, how many full-time employees at this company are actually holding down a part-time job of at least 10 hours per week. *(Rigorous) (Skill 12.4)*

A.   714

B.   625

C.   21,875

D.   28,571

Answer: C. 21,875

$\frac{35}{40}$ full time employees have a part time job also. Out of 25,000 full time employees, the number that also have a part time job is

$\frac{35}{40} = \frac{x}{25000} \rightarrow 40x = 875000 \rightarrow x = 21875$, so 21875 full time employees also have a part time job.

90.   Consider the following recipe ingredients for a dish that serves eight people:

one 3 ½-pound chicken
½ teaspoon of thyme
7 tablespoons butter

What would the correct amounts be to only serve 4 people? (Rigorous) (Skill 12.4)

   A.   1.6 pounds of chicken, ¼ teaspoon of thyme,
          3 ¾ tablespoons of butter

   B.   1.8 pounds of chicken, ¼ teaspoon of thyme,
          3 ½ tablespoons of butter

   C.   1 ¾ pounds of chicken, ¼ teaspoon of thyme,
          3 ½ tablespoons of butter

   D.   1 ¾ pounds of chicken, ¼ teaspoon of thyme,
          3 ¼ tablespoons of butter

Answer: C. 1 ¾ pounds of chicken, ¼ teaspoon of thyme,
              3 ½ tablespoons of butter

First, determine the conversion factor. Conversion Factor = $\dfrac{4}{8} = \dfrac{1}{2}$

Multiply each ingredient by the conversion factor.
        3 ½ X ½ =   1 ¾ pounds of chicken
        ½ x ½ =   ¼ teaspoon of thyme
        7 x ½ =   3 ½ tablespoons of butter

STATE MAJOR COMPONENTS RETAINED AND CHANGES OF IDEA 2004

The second revision of IDEA occurred in 2004, when IDEA was re-authorized as the Individuals with Disabilities Education Improvement Act of 2004 (IDEIA 2004). It is commonly referred to as IDEA 2004. IDEA 2004 was effective July 1, 2005.

It was the intention to improve IDEA by adding the philosophy and understanding that special education students need preparation for further study beyond the high school setting by teaching compensatory methods. Accordingly, IDEA 2004 provided a close tie to PL 89-10, the Elementary and Special Education Act of 1965, and stated that students with special needs should have maximum access to the general curriculum. This was defined as the amount for an individual student to reach his fullest potential. Full inclusion was stated not to be the only option by which to achieve this, and specified that skills should be taught to compensate students later in life in cases where inclusion was not the best setting.

IDEA 2004 added a new requirement for special education teachers on the secondary level enforcing NCLB's "Highly Qualified" requirements in the subject area of their curriculum. The rewording in this part of IDEA states that they shall be "no less qualified" than teachers in the core areas.

Free and Appropriate Public Education (FAPE) was revised by mandating that students have maximum access to appropriate general education. Additionally, LRE placement for those students with disabilities must have the same school placement rights as those students who are not disabled. IDEA 2004 recognizes that due to the nature of some disabilities, appropriate education may vary in the amount of participation/placement in the general education setting. For some students, FAPE will mean a choice as to the type of educational institution they attend (private school for example), any of which must provide the special education services deemed necessary for the student through the IEP.

The definition of *assistive technology devices* was amended to exclude devices that are surgically implanted (i.e. cochlear implants), and clarified that students with assistive technology devices shall not be prevented from having special education services. Assistive technology devices may need to monitored by school personnel, but schools are not responsible for the implantation or replacement of such devices surgically. An example of this would be a cochlear implant.

The definition of *child with a disability* is the term used for children ages 3-9 with a developmental delay now has been was changed to allow for the inclusion of Tourettes Syndrome.

IDEA 2004 recognized that all states must follow the National Instructional Materials Accessibility Standards which states that students who need materials in a certain form will get those at the same time their non-disabled peers receive their materials. Teacher recognition of this standard is important.

Changes in Requirements for Evaluations

The clock/time allowance between the request for an initial evaluation and the determination if a disability is present may be requested has been changed to state the finding/determination must occur within 60 calendar days of the request. This is a significant change as previously it was interpreted to mean 60 school days. Parental consent is also required for evaluations and prior to the start of special education services.

No single assessment or measurement tool may now be used to determine special education qualification. Assessments and measurements used should be in *language and form* that will give the most accurate picture of the child's abilities.

IDEA 2004 recognized that there exists a disproportionate representation of minorities and bilingual students and that pre-service interventions that are *scientifically based on early reading programs, positive behavioral interventions and support, and early intervening services* may prevent some of those children from needing special education services. This understanding has led to a child not being considered to have a disability if he/she has not had appropriate education in math or reading, nor shall a child be considered to have a disability if the reason for his/her delays is that English is a second language.

When determining a specific learning disability, the criteria may or may not use a discrepancy between *achievement and intellectual ability* but whether or not the child responds to scientific research-based intervention. In general, children who may not have been found eligible for special education (via testing) but are known to need services (via functioning, excluding lack of instruction) are still eligible for special education services. This change now allows input for evaluation to include state and local testing, classroom observation, academic achievement, and *related developmental need.*,

Changes in Requirements for IEPs

Individualized Education Plans (IEPS) continue to have multiple sections. One section, *present levels,* now addresses *academic achievement and functional performance.* Annual IEP goals must now address the same areas.

IEP goals should be aligned to state standards; thus short term objectives are not required on every IEP. Students with IEPs must not only participate in regular education programs to the full extent possible, they must show progress in those programs. This means that goals should be written to reflect academic progress.

For students who must participate in alternate assessment, there must be alignment to *alternate achievement standards.*

Significant change has been made in the definition of the IEP team as it now includes *not less than 1* teacher from each of the areas of special education and regular education be present.

IDEA 2004 recognized that the amount of required paperwork placed upon teachers of students with disabilities should be reduced if possible; for this reason a pilot program has been developed in which some states will participate using multi-year IEPs. Individual student inclusion in this program will require consent by both the school and the parent.

XAMonline, INC. 21 Orient Ave. Melrose, MA 02176

Toll Free number 800-509-4128

TO ORDER Fax 781-662-9268 OR www.XAMonline.com

NEW YORK STATE TEACHER CERTIFICATION
EXAMINATION   - NYSTCE - 2007

PO#   Store/School:

Address 1:

Address 2 (Ship to other):

City, State Zip

Credit card number_____-_____-_____-_____   expiration_____

EMAIL _____

PHONE   **FAX**

13# ISBN 2007	TITLE	Qty	Retail	Total
978-1-58197-866-7	NYSTCE ATS-W ASSESSMENT OF TEACHING SKILLS- WRITTEN 91			
978-1-58197-867-4	NYSTCE ATAS ASSESSMENT OF TEACHING ASSISTANT SKILLS 095			
978-1-58197-854-4	CST BIOLOGY 006			
978-1-58197-855-1	CST CHEMISTRY 007			
978-1-58197-865-0	CQST COMMUNICATION AND QUANTITATIVE SKILLS TEST 080			
978-1-58197-856-8	CST EARTH SCIENCE 008			
978-1-58197-851-3	CST ENGLISH 003			
978-1-58197-862-9	CST FAMILY AND CONSUMER SCIENCES 072			
978-1-58197-858-2	CST FRENCH SAMPLE TEST 012			
978-1-58197-868-1	LAST LIBERAL ARTS AND SCIENCE TEST 001			
978-1-58197-863-6	CST LIBRARY MEDIA SPECIALIST 074			
978-1-58197-861-2	CST LITERACY 065			
978-1-58197-852-0	CST MATH 004			
978-1-58197-872-8	CST MULTIPLE SUBJECTS 002 SAMPLE QUESTIONS			
978-1-58197-850-6	CST MUTIPLE SUBJECTS 002			
978-1-58197-864-3	CST PHYSICAL EDUCATION 076			
978-1-58197-857-5	CST PHYSICS SAMPLE TEST 009			
978-1-58197-853-7	CST SOCIAL STUDIES 005			
978-1-58197-859-9	CST SPANISH 020			
978-1-58197-860-5	CST STUDENTS WITH DISABILITIES 060			

		SUBTOTAL	
FOR PRODUCT PRICES VISIT WWW.XAMONLINE.COM	Ship	$8.25
	TOTAL	